Protestant Nation
The Fragile Christian Roots of America's Greatness

Other Books of Interest from St. Augustine's Press

Edward Feser, *The Last Superstition:*
A Refutation of the New Atheism

John F. Crosby and Stafford Betty, *What Does It Mean to Be a*
Christian?: A Debate between Orthodoxy and New Age Theology

St. Augustine, *The St. Augustine LifeGuide:*
Words to Live by from the Great Christian Saint

James V. Schall, *The Regensburg Lecture*

James V. Schall, *The Praise of 'Sons of Bitches':*
On the Worship of God by Fallen

John of Saint Thomas, *Introduction to the*
Summa Theologiae of Thomas Aquinas

Richard Watson, *The Philosophers Enigma: God, Body & Soul*

Leszek Kolakowski, *Religion If There Is No God . . .*

Leszek Kolakowski, *The Two Eyes of Spinoza:*
And Other Essays on Philosopher

Ralph C. Hancock, *Calvin and the Foundations of Modern Politics*

Pierre Manent, *Beyond Radical Secularism: How France and the*
Christian West Should Respond to the Islamic Challenge

Pierre Manent, *Seeing Things Politically:*
Interviews with Benedicte Delorme-Montini

Trevor Shelley, *Globalization and Liberalism:*
An Essay on Montesquieu, Tocqueville, and Manent

Klaus Vondung, *Paths to Salvation: The National Socialist Religion*

Peter Kreeft, *Ecumenical Jihad: Ecumenism and the Culture War*

Peter Kreeft, *An Ocean Full of Angel*

Josef Pieper, *Not Yet the Twilight: An Autobiography 1945–1964*

Josef Pieper, *Scholasticism:*
Personalities and Problems of Medieval Philosophy

Protestant Nation
The Fragile Christian Roots
of America's Greatness

Alain Besançon
Translated by Ralph C. Hancock

ST. AUGUSTINE'S PRESS
South Bend, Indiana

Library of Congress Control Number: 2018966669

∞ The paper used in this publication meets the minimum
requirements of the American National Standard for Information Sciences -
Permanence of Paper for Printed Materials, ANSI Z39.48-1984.

St. Augustine's Press
www.staugustine.net

My intention had been to write an essay on American Protestantism. I had already learned from experience, in writing on Russia, France, Islam, and on art, that nothing is comprehensible if one neglects the religious choices that determine a historical destiny. I was thus hoping for a better understanding of this complicated country where I had lived for three years.

The United States is the most powerful of the nations that divide the earth and one of the most religious. It is fundamentally Protestant. But this Protestantism was inherited from various European sources. The pilgrims of the Mayflower did not have to invent any new theologies; they already had some fully developed, each of which had a long history.

The result was that I could not approach the heart of my subject without first getting clear on the meaning of the various denominations and persuasions that give American piety its form. For this it was necessary to come back to Europe, understanding that it was not a question of a "mind-set" or of a "sensibility" as is said today, but indeed of a precise theology, argued and rational. Theology is a powerful auxiliary discipline that anyone who calls himself a historian had better know. Why did these pilgrims risk their lives on the high seas and among the Indians? Because they could not bear that Anglican prelates wore liturgical vestments?

This carried me further than I expected. I had to lengthen my title in order to take in Protestant history as a whole, but without forgetting my original intention, without looking away from the United States.

Along the way I noticed that the learned ones to whom I showed my manuscript were almost wholly ignorant of the question, which left them vulnerable to seeing the points of doctrine for which Europeans had slaughtered each other as no less foreign than Australian myths. However basic my essay may be, I hope it will teach readers (as it taught its author in writing it) some new things.

These are things I found prodigiously interesting. I believe, indeed, along with Bossuet, "that religion and civil government are the two hinges on which human affairs turn."

I.
PREHISTORY

September 11th

The shock of September 11, 2001 brought out a religious factor in the landscape of American politics to which Europeans had not paid much attention. The second election of President George W. Bush, according to the experts, turned more on questions of morality and religion than on economic questions.

I intend to examine the movement generally referred to as "evangelical," in itself, in its origins and in its relationship with other churches. I will not recount its history; others have already done this very well. But I would like to trace its theological logic. There is in fact a theological unity to Protestantism. As diverse, even fragmented as this movement may be, it recognizes itself and does not allow itself to be confused with Eastern churches and even less with Churches that accept Rome's jurisdiction. However well-disposed it may be toward them, this movement retains a very vivid sense of its borders, a point that merits our reflection.

The goal of this essay is both modest and ambitious. It is modest because it aims only to provide an elementary understanding of a movement that is so prominent in current affairs. Our age grants a certain importance to the phenomenon of religion only if it shows up in the news. It sees only the external features and does not try to understand anything about religion but the passions that it inspires and the behaviors by which it attests. We do not feel the need to examine the reasons religion gives, because, for the contemporary mind, it belongs entirely to the domain of the irrational, alongside fashion, rock music, jogging and other such manifestations. The fact that one is Catholic, Baptist, Methodist, or Muslim is wholly a matter of taste, or at least of individual choice, which is legitimate and recognized and protected by the democratic state. If theological culture was more widespread, rather than being relegated to the outer darkness where a few specialists continue to operate, we would better understand that we belong to one confession or another because there are good reasons for belonging to it. The diversity of confessions would seem less arbitrary if we had learned to recognize that it originates in certain great intellectual decisions that then develop and ramify according to their own logic, or, if you will, their own particular genetic codes. If Protestants recognize each other, it is because they are aware of their dependence on first principles that were developed over four centuries in a way that was sufficiently homogeneous. To trace this development is to better understand history, because theological options make a difference in practice and are a penetrating key—though not the only one—to explanation. This is the logic I would like to grasp. I am aware that this is an ambitious goal.

Two Challenges

Since the Vatican II Council, the Catholic Church has seen two great challenges grow before it, and has been in no hurry to become aware of them.

The first is Islam, concerning which we are still talking in terms of "dialogue," "openness," or "reconciliation," which suggests that we have still not taken its measure. The ignorance of Islam, of its religious structure, of its specific relation to the God of Israel is massive. One evidence of this is the usage, even by clerics of the first rank, of defective expressions such as "the three Abrahamic religions" (the fact that Islam claims to belong to the faith of Abraham does not prove that it professes it authentically), or "the three religions of the Book." But since this latter expression has a meaning in Islam that has nothing to do with what Christians have in mind, its use is simply an indication of ignorance. If Christians have become incapable of seeing the difference between this religion and their own, the border that separates them is becoming porous and easier to cross.

The second challenge is that of a new advance by the Reformation, in unprecedented forms that need to be analyzed.

I have just alluded to conversions from Catholicism to Islam. They are plentiful in Africa, but still rare in Europe, even though many preconditions are in place for them to become numerous. On the other hand, there are already massive conversions in the direction of the new versions of Protestantism. This is true not only in Africa and in Latin America, but also in the United States and soon in Europe. And what is more, the themes and the leading ideas of this reform are penetrating inside Catholic churches and are there bringing forth organizations, ways of being, and new forms of religiosity the provenance and confessional tenor of which these churches do not seem to recognize.

These two challenges should not be considered of the same order. In the case of Islam it is a matter of another religion, one that was born as a deliberate and conscious refusal of Christianity and whose principles are radically incompatible with its own. With the new Reformed religiosity, it is a matter among Christians. It must be repeatedly affirmed that Methodists, Pentecostals, Baptists, and the millions of believers divided up among hundreds of churches are Christians. They were baptized and their baptism is perfectly valid in the eyes of Catholics. On all sides there is an ardent desire for unity, which is an inseparable component of the common faith, and most are subject to a more or less precise ecumenical aspiration. It must also be noted that the old forms of Protestantism, faithful to the exact tradition of Luther and of Calvin, are affected as much as Catholicism by the new currents. Still the old and the new remain in solidarity. They are still within the sphere of Protestantism. This is not the case for Catholics who remain separated from the Reformation confessions by a precise border, of which the Protestants retain an awareness that is perhaps even stronger than what the "papists" experience toward them.

What is new is that this border is moving.

For a long time it was stable. In the first century of the Reformation, the borders were mobile and penetrable. France, where perhaps twenty percent of the population favored the Reformation, and whose elites, more drawn to it than were the people, were very close to taking power, turned again toward Catholicism following dramatic events such as the St. Bartholomew's Day Massacre and thirty years of cruel war. In the aftermath of the Edict of Nantes the Protestants retained some modest positions. The Revocation drove them out, but, as Pierre Chaunu believed, this perhaps produced a reaction that saved Protestantism when it was on the verge of exhaustion.

It was during the Thirty Years War that the matter was settled definitively. Wallenstein's armies had reconquered almost all of North Germany and the Catholic hierarchy had been reestablished in the great ports of the Baltic, essential bases of the Reformation. The king of England, James I, dreamed of rejoining Rome. According to Ranke, this is the moment when Pope Urban VIII, worried about the power of the Habsburgs and concerned for his papal domains in Italy, pulled the rug out from under Wallenstein. Following this, the Imperial Army disbanded, leaving the field open to Gustave-Adolphe in a stunning Protestant counteroffensive supported by Richelieu. After ten years of horrible war and destruction, the border was more or less settled in the middle of Germany. At the same time the Jesuits almost succeeded in bringing the Poles back to Catholicism, and, to a lesser degree, the Hungarians and the Czechs.

In any case, around 1640 the boundaries stopped moving. There is no more switching from one church to another. "The religious map of Europe is now set in stone" (Chaunu). The proportion of Catholics and of Protestants is no longer affected by conversions, which are henceforth individual and rare, but by demographic variations that arise in the respective and relatively homogeneous zones of the two confessions. Until recently, this proportion hovered around 2/3 to 1/3—two-thirds Catholic and one-third Protestant. Each of the two factions of Christianity had refined its own apologetic argument. They had forged their weapons, completed their defensive systems, and reinforced their armor. In the mixed zones, they had learned to cohabit without mingling. They were no longer a threat; the states had taken this cohabitation into account and enacted laws to organize it, to prevent conflicts, and to ensure freedom of worship and freedom of thought.

Now it seems that this proportion is changing. In Africa and in Latin America there are whole swaths of the Catholic church that are going over to these new churches that call themselves evangelical. These churches are animated by a fearless missionary dynamism that dares, without fear and with some success, to take on the massive presence of Islam, previously untouched by traditional Christian missionary activity. The result is that the church of Rome, after all the challenges it has had to confront in the last two centuries—democracy, anti-democracy, ideological totalitarianisms, and today the challenge of Islam that is coming to the fore—must now confront a new Reformation that is awakening from a long sleep.

This Reformation cannot however be described in the framework of the Reformation of the sixteenth century. The professions of faith published by the various denominations have not changed; they refer to the principles of the great reformers. They accept and confess the Nicene Creed. They are Trinitarian, and only rarely Unitarian. They believe in salvation through Jesus Christ. They are faithful to the great inaugural affirmations: *sola fide, sola scriptura, sola gratia.* What is new is a change of emphasis.

The "notes" that determine the character of the church have in principle been preserved: one, holy, Catholic, apostolic, as these are set forth in the creed professed by most religious groupings posterior to the Reformation. To be sure these notes are understood differently in the Protestant world and in the Catholic world. But what is new is that other notes are being added. The new churches are *affective, non-dogmatic, associative, moralizing, democratic,* and *civic.* These new notes, which are not a matter of dogma, and are not even thematized, allow us to describe the new situation. It is these that exert a greater and greater attraction on the Roman church. How did they become established? To grasp this we must go back a long way, to the origins of the Reformation.

Christianity Is an Intellectual and Affective Religion

The affective side has always been important in Christianity as in every other religion. Christianity mobilizes the human being in all his or her faculties. The very person of Jesus Christ touches the heart of the disciples: "did not our hearts burn within us as he spoke to us on the road and explained the Scriptures to us?" (Luke 24:32) "Heart" does not only mean here the central point, the metaphysical point where the essence of the person is concentrated, but the site of an affective, emotional experience, the sensory organ of the emotions, of suffering, of love.

Nevertheless, in the first Christian centuries, it is not the affective faculties that are highlighted. The accent is put on the knowledge of God. "And this is life eternal, that they might know thee the only true God, and Jesus Christ, whom thou hast sent." (John 17:3) And here is St. Paul: "For now we see through a glass, darkly; but then face to face: now I know in part; but then shall I know even as also I am known." (I Corinthians 13:12) How is this knowledge to be obtained? By the mediation of Scripture, by contemplation of the creation, by holy images, by mysteries, by rational effort to understand faith, and, at the summit, by the mystical contemplation of God. The contemplative effort of Christianity is in no way opposed to the exercise of contemplation as recommended by philosophy. Contemplation has crowned philosophic life since Plato and Aristotle, and on through the Stoics and Neoplatonists who give the first generations of Christianity their conceptual equipment. It becomes part of Christian spiritual life as a superior form of intellectual vision, the fulfillment of the natural and supernatural desire to know God, and more generally as the highest human activity.

Contemplation is also a matter of love. But we love only what we know. This is why the primacy of knowledge over will (the faculty of love) is upheld by the church fathers and in classical scholasticism. Knowledge in its properly Christian understanding is the deepening of this "truth of life" that is the mystery of Christ, contemplated in the Scriptures (Old and New Testaments), in light of the tradition and in liturgical celebration. This knowledge develops within each person along with "the love of God spread abroad in our hearts by the Holy Spirit" (Romans 5:5) Each nourishes the other, since love is guided and channeled by knowledge. This is why the Alexandrians speak of "gnosis," referring not to the surrounding Gnosticism, which they considered a false gnosis, and still less to a Hellenic contamination, as modern Protestant theologians (Harnack, for example) have often thought, but rather owing to the propaedeutic role that the tradition of Greek philosophy can play in the acquisition of this knowledge.

This intellectual instrument, as well as the beginnings of a scientific exegesis in this same city of Alexandria, creates a tension within knowledge between theology, which becomes more and more technical, and mysticism. This latter term, which once applied to the study of the Scriptures and to the sacramental life of the church, is later applied, following pseudo-Dionysus to a *pati divina*, that is, a feeling of the "presence" (Gregory of Nyssa) or of the "experience" of the living God in the intimacy of the soul. Still, in the thought of Evagrius Ponticus and that of John Cassian the traditional meaning of *gnosis* (in Latin, *scientia*) is maintained as a whole that brings together indivisibly all the possible degrees, from the simple faith of the baptized Christian to the mystical exercises in which one savors a foretaste of the beatific life. Augustine sometimes reserves *scientia* to theology and instead gives the name *sapientia* to the living knowledge of divine realities. For St. Thomas, one cannot have one without the other; there can be no theology without the light of faith.

At the apogee of the thirteenth century, for example in the thought of St. Thomas Aquinas, the various faculties find a certain precarious equilibrium. Theological science satisfies the intellect; liturgy and collective piety give Christian experience a social base; spiritual life, even when it attains a mystical intensity, does not rupture the unity of the person, and carries it entire toward divine contemplation. In the next century a dissociation will arise.

The Nominalist Revolution

It is a surprising fact that the Thomistic synthesis—so accomplished, apparently so stable— was contested and demolished in such a short time. Thomas Aquinas had only just died, his body was still warm, and already this contestation and demolition was being carried out by Christian thinkers of the first rank. The contemplation to which Thomas invited the reader was directed toward a hierarchical world, where everything was ordered by degrees, from a rock up to God. The means of this ordering was the idea of analogy. According to this idea, there existed between things in the world a relationship of proportion, but the absolute disproportion between the world and its creator left open a means for maintaining the scale that holds them together: analogy. God is beyond goodness, but he is good. He is beyond Being, but he Is.

Duns Scotus's innovation was to introduce a separation between theology and philosophy. As Etienne Gilson remarks, "after a brief medieval honeymoon, theology and philosophy seem to realize that their marriage was a mistake. While awaiting a physical separation, which will come before long, the parties proceed to a separation of property. Each side reclaims possession of its problems and forbids the other to touch them."

It is difficult to pass judgment on Duns Scotus, and I will not attempt it. What was he really trying to say? The Dominican tradition is hard on him. The Franciscan tradition sees him as its main master. The magisterium of the Church has not committed itself either for or against his doctrine. The learned are divided where he is concerned. Should we see him on Saint Thomas's side, or on William of Ockham's?

For metaphysics to be possible, according to Duns Scotus, it must be given as an object a notion of being so abstract and indeterminate that it can be applied indifferently to everything that is, to things and to God himself. Analogy, or the equivocacy of being, the cornerstone of Thomism, is thus contested. This is what he calls the univocity of being. The paradox is that at the same time God's transcendence is reduced by the principle of univocity, this same transcendence is reestablished in another way, and in a discouraging manner, by the affirmation of the incomprehensibility of the divine being.

Heaven becomes farther away, since God is no longer really grasped except by revelation, and the proofs of his existence and many of his attributes are no longer accessible to natural metaphysical reason, at least in beginning with sense experience. Scotus takes up and "colors" Saint Anselm's proof, which Thomas had rejected. For him, there is no real separation between essence and existence, and thus it is the essence of God to exist. But his relation to the world is no longer either defined or determinate. This is another feature of Thomism: its insistence on divine freedom and on the contingency of its effects. It does all it can to lift God up above his ideas, and then, in order effectively to guarantee the rupture, it separates the creature from the Creator by the decree of a supreme freedom. The will of God is the absolute master of choice and of the combination of created essences. It is not subjected to the rule of the Good: "It is on the contrary the rule of the good that is subjected to it." A thing is good because God has willed it.

As a compensation, the earth comes nearer. The universality of the species fragments into diverse individuals. For Thomas, the Aristotelian, all things are composed of form and matter, and individuation is brought about by primal matter. For Scotus, individuation is from nature. The individual is a positive entity, the final reality at once of form, of matter, and of the composite thing. This *entitas singularis*, or *haecceitas*, endows the individual with the seal that makes of it a being. In addition to being composed of form and of matter, the human being is human by virtue of the *haecceitas*.

Ockham takes the criticism initiated by the Subtle Doctor to the limit. His is thus much clearer. For Ockham, certain knowledge is knowledge that is immediately evident. Intuitive knowledge, what is simply given, alone allows us to reach the facts, to reach existing things. It is the sole starting point of experiential knowledge. The field of philosophy must thus be cleared of essences and of the imaginary causes that encumber it. The only way to prove that one thing is caused by another is to have recourse to experience and to verify that, if a cause is not posited, the effect does not happen.

When we say "the man is running," it is not "man" who is running, but a person. When we say "man is a species," "man" does not mean an individual, but a community. Is there really something that corresponds to this community, to this universal? No. All that is real outside of thought is an individual. The genus and species are nothing outside of thought. Individuals can be classified, and that is all there is. Terms that we call general concepts designate individuals in a confused way. Terms that designate things signify the same objects, but distinctly known. There is no reason to suppose some intermediary between the thing itself and the mind, no more than we need to introduce an intermediary (an idea) between the God who creates and the things that he creates. It is understandable that when Ockham applies these principles to the classic problems of natural theology he finds only doubtful responses. This theologian thus relegates what is essential in metaphysics to theology and to answers supplied by revelation and by faith.

Thus he rejects the "proofs" of the existence of God. The proof by the prime mover is based on the impossibility of tracing the causes of motion in an infinite series. And yet nothing prevents us from supposing that this series is infinite. Moreover, the principle according to which everything that moves is moved by something else is not evident: an angel moves itself, the soul moves itself. The idea that God is one and infinite is probable. It cannot be held as certain. Nor do we know his attributes: that he is all-powerful, that he is the supreme being, these things we know by faith, but we are incapable of demonstrating them. We know by direct experience such things as joy and sadness. But the soul as a substance or the agent intellect escapes us completely.

It is in the domain of morality that Ockham prepares the future Reformation. Moral laws are subject to the pure and simple will of God. The hatred of God, theft, and adultery are wrong because of the divine precept that forbids them. But God might have prescribed them as meritorious acts. He does not have to reward merits, nor to punish faults. He can condemn the innocent and save the guilty. Since universal archetypes and essences have been eliminated, nothing can contain the divine arbitrary will. God is disconnected from wisdom.

What religious concern in the mind of this Franciscan could have led him to such an overturning, such an obliteration of the hard-won accomplishment of the theology of the thirteenth century? No doubt it was a reaction against the necessitarianism of Greek philosophy, both Platonic and Aristotelian, which this great theology had assimilated while limiting it. Ockham is always reminding the reader of the first article of the Creed: "*Credo in unum Deum, Patrem omnipotentem.*" No doubt the "*Omnipotens*" did not have exactly the same meaning as the *Pantocrator* of the Greek Creed. It overlooks all that was implied in the *Patrem* that qualifies the *Omnipotentia*, that is, the Father's fundamental benevolence toward his creation and toward his creature, man. Ockham's God is not the God of Avicenna, whose will necessarily follows the law of his intellect. It is a God who obeys nothing, not even the ideas, for there are no ideas in God, any more than there is a universal in things.

Everything is therefore contingent in Ockham's universe. Everything hangs on God's *potential absoluta*. There is nothing that could not have been otherwise if he had so decided. He can always produce an effect without bothering with secondary causes. He can even make it so that we have sensory intuition of things that do not exist. Things in our world happen in a certain way; this is a simple matter of fact. Here we are in a world that evokes the world of Islam where suspicion always hovers over the reality of events that obey only the "habits" of God, which he can change at any moment.

Ockham is not alone and his originality is contested. He is simply the foremost and the most brilliant thinker of the movement of thought that will dominate the fourteenth century and beyond. Some of his disciples are still more radical. Nicholas of Autrecourt proceeds to a critique of causality that prefigures Hume. From the existence of one thing one cannot conclude the existence of another. The link that binds the cause to the effect is neither necessary nor evident. It must be verified empirically, by experience.

The intellectual fruits of "nominalism" are numerous. The most distinctive is perhaps the enormous development of logic, whose exercises of ever greater subtlety, virtuosity, and sterility occupy what is called "decadent" scholasticism, but whose ingeniousness and worth have been rediscovered in our day. The most remarkable fruit is its opening the path of modern science. Since things are separated, since no order binds them together, it is not possible to discover their arrangement without submitting them to observation and experience. The omnipotence of God, of an inaccessible God whose intentions and acts of will one cannot know *a priori*, is such that it becomes necessary to rely on sciences of observation. It is no longer possible to understand reality according to immutable models and eternal ideas. One must go and see, and in order to do this one must look in another direction, one must be converted to things. Thus it very soon becomes obvious that things are not as we thought in the Aristotelian-Thomist tradition. They thought they knew much, almost everything, and they find that they know almost nothing and that the whole tradition is disqualified. From this point of view the revolution of the fourteenth century is perhaps the most important in the intellectual history of the West, if we consider, along with Gilson, that the great rationalist and scientific mutation of the seventeenth century rests on metaphysical positions that were affirmed or sketched three centuries earlier. Contemporary neo-Thomism groans under the destructive effects of the nominalism that swept aside or ruptured the great tradition that went from Plato to St. Thomas. It is aware that Christian reason, even reason pure and simple, has never recovered the stable basis that it once enjoyed. Regarding this loss, which is certainly enormous, we must nevertheless consider what this revolution has made possible. Without it, we would have to renounce automobiles, the telephone, word processing, Tylenol, etc.—that is, millions of things that make up the modern world. This is not tenable. The problem would be to recover within this infinite and amorphous multiplicity the meaning of being in its ordered and unifying hierarchy that fulfilled the aspirations of the ancients. But this problem has not been resolved.

Let us however take a closer look at the religious effects.

Ockham, Nicholas of Autrecourt, John of Mirecourt, and Nicolas Oresme were mendicant monks and theologians. There is no doubt concerning their Catholic faith. But since metaphysics no longer brings any comfort, they need to fall back on the Holy Science. Theology contains all that is necessary for salvation. It is to this science that we must turn in order to answer the questions and address the torments of the Christian soul. But it can no longer count on any philosophic demonstration. This drives thought inevitably toward the regime of the double truth, and finally to skepticism coupled with fideism, which is a classic combination.

Pierre Chaunu notes that the alchemist movement corresponds with the catastrophes of the fourteenth century and the ruin of the beautiful certitudes of the century of Saint Louis and of Saint Thomas. The world appears unpredictable and truly contingent. All systems that aim to link the universe with a predictable structure seem, after the black plague, devoid of meaning. This century of cataclysms is at the same time a century of little steps in technical progress, fruits of initiative, individual freedom, groping and chance. The free, impenetrable, and unpredictable God guides humanity according to a plan of salvation that is revealed only in the Bible and nowhere else.

In the area of spiritual life, something seems to be definitively lost, the unity of contemplation. There was once a felicitous concordance of all the faculties. The intelligence was fulfilled by what it discovered little by little in the depths of the Christian mystery. The will, that is love, was inflamed by this same discovery. Henceforth the intellect is frustrated and itself ratifies this frustration. The will, no longer guided by knowledge, makes its way in uncertainty, and finds itself in a sphere of unknown contours. And yet it must find a way to orient itself.

Varieties of Speculative Mysticism

If we limit ourselves to what actually happened in history, it seems that only a small number of directions were available to choose from. These were, successively or simultaneously, the return to the old mystical speculation of late antiquity, the imaginary flights of the Gnostics, millenarian outbursts, simple piety without philosophic pretension, and finally the recourse to Holy Scripture, *sola scriptura.*

In the writings of Eckhart, a Dominican, the love of God, this impassioned love that drives the mystical life, takes a new path. Yet it is not so new, considering that it resembles a Christian renewal of the Neoplatonic mysticism of Plotinus and Proclus, but stripped of the Aristotelian elements that the prudence and the realism of Albert the Great and St. Thomas had brought to it. Here again— but in a different way than in nominalism—God is projected to a distance still further than that indicated by the enigmatic *ego sum qui sum* (I am that I am) of Scripture. He is beyond being. In effect being is appropriate only to creatures and has no place in God but as its cause. God is higher than being, he is pure of all being. He is the One. As an Orthodox Christian, Eckhart distinguishes in God the unitary essence and the three persons. But even higher than essence, at the summit of all, resides the "purity" of the immobile unity. Divinity resides beyond the divine persons.

"If God is being because he is One, and if nothing besides God is one, then nothing besides him is being" (Gilson). This means that creatures are pure nothings, *nulleitas*. The nominalist exploration of the world is of no interest. Eckhart retreats to the soul. Augustinian psychology distinguished three main faculties in the soul: memory, intellect, and will. They are created, because they are part of the created soul. Eckhart discerns a deeper, uncreated, properly divine element. He calls it the "citadel" or the "spark" of the soul, one and simple as is the One. The human effort to unite with God thus turns toward the most profoundly internal and attempts to find refuge in the "citadel" where it is one with God. Here Eckhart is very close to the Hesychast mysticism of the Eastern Church. Having attained this point, man can renounce interest in the rest. External acts are neutral, neither good nor bad. Creatures are pure nothingness, except for the soul, because it contains what leads back to God himself. Once isolated in the citadel, the soul detaches from itself, abandons itself, and attains its pure essence, its freedom. This is why poverty is the highest virtue: the soul no longer possesses anything, nor knows anything, nor desires anything, because it has only to desire what it already possesses. We find in Eckhart a glorification of an absolute disinterestedness that prepares the "impossible supposition" (indifference to hell itself) of later authors. If man strips himself of all desire, even the most noble (his salvation), when he approaches God in absolute disinterestedness, then we have attained the "pure love" of Fenelon three centuries in advance. Prayer of supplication is inconceivable. Faith, grace, and sacraments are secondary. These are preparations, steps on a ladder (Cognet). The feeling of an individual face-to-face between the believer and God, the depreciation of ecclesiastical mediations and the reliance of religious consciousness on the inward soul— these are all features that will survive in the Reformation.

We find, at the heart of the most incontestable orthodoxy, in the thought of Tauler, the idea of a "summit" or "ground" of the soul. But the doctrine takes on a *psychological* form. Between the ground of the soul and its faculties a properly affective element intervenes, the *Gemüt*. The *Gemüt* is a stable condition of the heart that regulates all the faculties, for better or for worse. If the believer turns toward the ground of the soul, then all is well, for there he finds God. If not, he turns away from Him. Still, Tauler does not hold that this mystical contemplation is sufficient. He recommends the exercise of the virtues, and not only for propaedeutic reasons. He assumes quite literally Saint Bonaventure's formula and the *soul's journey into God*: the only path that leads to the end is the imitation of Jesus Christ.

This is the case more clearly, and within a simpler and calmer body of thought, in the ideas of Ruysbroeck; here Neoplatonist speculation becomes almost invisible. This is philosophy. He situates himself in the line of Saint Bernard. The path of unity does not lead man to isolate himself in the inner fortress where pure divinity is found, but rather, in a more classical tradition, to seek God through the mediation of Christ, the image in which he was created, his eternal exemplar. Tauler and Ruysbroeck are favored authors in Protestant spirituality, as we will see.

Gnosticism

Faith seeks intelligence. Classical scholasticism had given intelligence the means to respond to faith's queries. It had set precise limits on what intelligence could attain by its own means, leaving the highest objects, the great Christian mysteries, to reveal and clarify themselves by their own means, more or less obscurely, in the sacred texts. The nominalist revolution considerably reduced the theoretical capacity of human reason to comprehend the truths of faith. These truths are returned to revealed theology. It also compensated by opening up the immense field of natural reality. But the Christian soul does not renounce the desire to know. Thus arises once again the gnostic temptation.

There is nothing new in this temptation. Since ancient times it has promised the initiated not only the partial knowledge of philosophy, but a total knowledge, or a central vision capable of integrating everything. Transcendent realities, physical phenomena, and historical events find in it a place and an explanation. Scholastic reason stops at a certain point. Nominalist reason stops even earlier. In one beat of its wings Gnosticism surpasses these limits and locates itself at the heart of divine understanding.

Ancient forms of Gnosticism resembled complicated metaphysical novels, including various celestial characters. Under Christianity it takes a considerably simpler form. Certain constants remain: the struggle between good and bad principles, and the three temporal stages: the past, or the separation of principles; the present, or their mixing; and the future, or the final victory of the good God. There is always the contempt for matter, for the flesh, begetting, and marriage; the rejection of the Old Testament and of its God. And there is still the pronounced separation between the initiated who know the gnostic program, the Perfect Ones, and the ordinary people whom the initiates must pull out of their ignorance and lead to salvation.

But Gnosticism is rarely seen in its pure form. It remains close to Christianity and draws strength from it (see Valentin). It borrows Christianity's vocabulary, its theological equipment, and its exegetical methods. It presents itself as a purer and higher form of Christianity, and its adherents strive to show it in the purity of their lives. It was rare for it to be caught *in flagrante delicto* of heresy, and it was ready to accept the most strict dogmatic professions, on the condition of understanding them within the framework of its own system. This was the way of the Bogomiles, the Patarines, and the Cathars.

The Church, at its height in the thirteenth century, had more or less contained the gnostic movements. It repressed them ferociously and with attention to detail. It discouraged them by proposing a superior and balanced doctrine fit to ensure some degree of intellectual peace. The crisis of this doctrine, the crisis of authority contemporaneous with the Great Schism of the West, provoked a return.

Should Gnosticism be classified with the kind of "leftism" that troubles the world of Western Christianity at the end of the Middle Ages? This is a mixture of millennialist ideas along with a rigorism of absolute poverty. In the thought of Joachim of Fiore we find the theme of the three ages: the age of the Father, of the law, of matter; the age of the Son, that is, the present, intermediary age, under the guidance of the Church; which will disappear and give way to a third age, that of the Holy Spirit, to be overseen by the initiates of the eternal Gospel, the members of the "order of the Righteous." The Church, and Rome, are the beast of the Apocalypse, the great whore. In the Low Countries these ideas nourish the Brothers of the Free Spirit, the Beghards and the Beguines, and, in Italy, the Franciscan *spirituali* and the *fraticelli*.

Contempt for the world wins over society. We are familiar with the macabre sensibility of the fifteenth century, the obsession with death. The Satanism of this time can be understood as an uprising of the evil principle. A wondrous interest in the diabolic is born, a whole people of sorcerers and witches who finally exhaust the patience of tribunals toward the middle of the seventeenth century. Clearly Christianity is in a black mood. It cannot be appeased by gnostic and paragnostic recipes. The rebellious and aberrant hyperintellectualism exasperates the affective malaise. But Gnosticism will continue to attract and to deceive adherents down to our day among those who hope, ever in vain, for a cure by some superior knowledge. It is the age-old compensation for ignorance or for philosophy's impotence and for dissatisfaction with faith, even faith supported by theology. Gnosticism in its many forms changes along with the world and attaches itself to Christianity as its shadow. It is one of its fundamental deviations.

Devotio Moderna

Nevertheless, in the fourteenth century a fourth path comes to light in England and in the Low Countries, the *devotio moderna*. It first presents itself as a rejection of speculative thought and in certain cases as an expression of a fatigue of intellectual life. Gerard of Groote has read the Rhenish mystics Ruysbroeck and Suso. He thinks he can keep them at arm's length. Contemplation is losing its intellectual aspect. He does not describe it. The only thing that counts is the requirement of divesting oneself, the *spiritualis paupertas,* the actual practice of the virtues and the perfection of charity. Charity is assimilated to contemplation: *contemplacio seu perfeccio caritatis.* In practice this amounts to imitating Christ in his humanity. This imitation is the essence of contemplation, but the active life is another form of contemplation. Let us note in passing this equivalence between the two lives, active and contemplative; in the Reformation this will be established (Vandenbroucke). This same pursuit of evangelical simplicity, of the soul's repose, inspires the Beguines who live peacefully, serenely and sweetly in their convents. We envision them, or others like them, in the paintings of Memling, on their knees, hands clasped together, an attentive eye fixed on the Virgin and her Son.

The masterpiece of this form of spirituality is Thomas a Kempis's work, *The Imitation of Christ.* Kempis lived this life of simplicity and methodical devotion for more than eighty years. The book stayed alive throughout the Western Christian world, Catholic as well as Protestant, to the point of being the most widely diffused work after the Bible. It is a collection designed to nourish the prayer of young canons in the Abby of Mont-Sainte-Agnés. It is a lesson in affective devotion through the contemplation of Christ's humanity, in order finally to be joined to God in the liberation of the soul. This contemplation is humble, "lateral, modest, and obscure." It is never identified with the blessed vision. For *The Imitation,* spiritual life is accessible to all. It becomes equivalent to the inner life; it involves discerning the movements of the soul of those who have decided to follow Christ.

"Spiritual life" is a relatively new term. Spiritual life in the *devotia moderna* is not the life of the mind. A gulf separates post-Ockham scholastic thought from the new spiritual masters and isolates theology-science in the life of the soul. The soul is essentially the seat of love, of a de-intellectualized love, a love felt by intense experience. It is called to live in emotion, in tender and affective devotion, which no long bothers to reflect on itself; passive, it sees itself as opening directly upon the divine. This can lead to a life of prayer, which the Spanish masters will give a more solid form, not without drawing upon the Rhenish-Flemish masters. This can also lead to the condition of a simple soul, soft complacency, passivity, valued for itself—what will later be called, as a direct descendent of *devotion moderna,* "pietism." Here religious consciousness is limited to a merely psychological reaction to the objects of belief, a reaction that can remain separate from or ignorant of its objects. It renounces the goal of attaining "real apprehension of what it believes" (Newman). Here we are already with Schleiermacher! If spiritual theology is not based on dogmatic theology, laying hold on what is given in theology by relating theology's content to religious consciousness, then spiritual theology is fated to degenerate into pietism (Bouyer). There is no *sapientia* without *scientia,* as Augustine would say.

Biblicism

The Imitation of Christ is a collection of Biblical citations, mostly from the Gospels, Psalms, the Wisdom Books, and Paul's epistles. Man finds nourishment not in bread alone, and still less in the vertiginous logical treatises produced in abundance by the Sorbonne or by Oxford, but in the Word that falls from the mouth of God. It is to be expected that the internal, solitary and individual piety of devout moderns would seek a guide and an incontestable domain. Where would this be found if not in the Bible?

The Bible is the property of the Church. It is within the Church that it was written, and it was the Church that gathered new Scriptures together with old, that fixed the Canon, and that gave it supreme authority on questions of doctrine. In the West, it provided the Vulgate, a good, stable and canonical version. It proclaimed the unity of this library of disparate books, written over 1000 years. It also provided the rules of interpretation: *littera gesta docet, quid credas allegoria, moralis quid agas, quo tendas anagogia* —that is, a distinction between the literal meaning, the allegorical meaning, the moral (tropological) meaning, and the anagogic meaning, that is, the meaning in relation to last things. For each meaning it provided its appropriate theological commentary.

We must doubtless recognize, following Pierre Chaunu, the great importance of the two treatises published by Wycliffe, both in 1378, *De veritate Scripturae sancta* and *De Ecclesia*. They affirm the supreme authority of Scripture, which is equivalent to removing it from the magisterium of the church. The Church, through its commentary and exegesis, in practice exercised a kind of tutelary role, at the limit a judgment.

Henceforth, citing the grave failings of the Church before its highest tribunal, the judgment of Scripture, Wycliffe, a century and a half before Luther, had understood that there existed, in the bosom of the Church, an irrecusable "possibility of appeal," the recourse to the irrecusable citation of the Word of God.

The modern believer reads the Bible all alone. He can read it because it is printed. In this "spiritual" reading he takes no account of theology; rather he tastes the poetic scripture that speaks to his heart and dispenses him from the systematic exposition of truth. His perspicacity is attached to the letter, which he would hold to be absolutely certain and authentic. This is why the first best-seller of the sixteenth century is Erasmus's New Testament, the *Novum Instrumentum* of 1516. From this moment philological research becomes a continuous and interminable effort, because the ardent Christian hopes that he will finally possess the very Word of God, stripped of all mistakes and additions.

In the great era of stone cathedrals, the cathedral of knowledge seemed to be completed. Bonaventure, Albert the Great, and Thomas Aquinas had constructed an intellectual edifice that rose to the height of religious consciousness, proper to satisfy the rational requirements of faith. This edifice was thrown down in very little time, thus leaving religious feeling to its own devices and the will to attain God through love without guidance. The contemplation in its dual nature, composed of intelligence and of will, was broken by the failure of its intellectual part. What then subsists are the powers of affectivity, piety, and indeed pietism, which no longer clings to anything but the Word of God such as it has been recorded in the Bible. This Word therefore becomes the object of passionate investigation. The stage is set for Luther's entrance.

II.
THE REFORMATION

Luther

But I, blameless monk that I was, felt that before God I was a sinner with an extremely troubled conscience. I couldn't be sure that God was appeased by my satisfaction. I did not love, no, rather I hated the just God who punishes sinners. In silence, if I did not blaspheme, then certainly I grumbled vehemently and got angry at God. I said, "Isn't it enough that we miserable sinners, lost for all eternity because of original sin, are oppressed by every kind of calamity through the Ten Commandments? Why does God heap sorrow upon sorrow through the Gospel and through the Gospel threaten us with his justice and his wrath?" This was how I was raging with wild and disturbed conscience. I constantly badgered St. Paul about that spot in Romans 1 and anxiously wanted to know what he meant.

I meditated night and day on those words until at last, by the mercy of God, I paid attention to their context: "The justice of God is revealed in it, as it is written: 'The just person lives by faith.'" I began to understand that in this verse the justice of God is that by which the just person lives by a gift of God, that is by faith. I began to understand that this verse means that the justice of God is revealed through the Gospel, but it is a

passive justice, i.e. that by which the merciful God justifies us by faith, as it is written: "The just person lives
by faith." All at once I felt that I had been born again
and entered into paradise itself through open gates. Immediately I saw the whole of Scripture in a different
light. (Lorz)

This is the account of the "tower experience" of Wittenberg,
which probably happened in 1513. Luther had been in hell for several years. His suffering was so intense, he wrote, that he could not
express it in words. And now his crisis resolves in a few moments.
A new form of Christianity has just appeared, one that springs
whole from the sudden resolution, in a solitary individual consciousness, of an acute existential crisis.

There has been endless examination of the psychological aspects, neurotic or other, of this mental suffering. Erickson wrote
about it from a psychiatric point of view. This kind of analysis
tends to lay Luther down in the Procrustean bed of ordinary neu-
rosis. But he is one of the strongest and most prodigiously gifted
personalities that humanity has produced; he is not a person to
confine to a poor "Oedipus complex." If he became the Reformer,
this is because of the coincidence between his exceptional personality and the reforming theological solutions that were available
to him.

He had little philosophical knowledge and experience; nothing
compared with his investment in and passion for reading the Bible.
In his monastery he was responsible for teaching, and his teaching
evinced an uncommon force and penetration. Every page taught
him God's transcendence. He thought that the faculty of knowledge
dispensed to man was hardly superior to the animals' and that,
where the knowledge of God is concerned, we have at our disposal
only what he has chosen to say of himself in his Word. When he
had nevertheless to account conceptually for this transcendence, he
fell back on the philosophy of his times – that is, on Ockham, and
more directly on the attenuated Ockhamism provided by Gabriel
Biel.

The sense of God as an irritable judge was something Luther had found in his bad conscience and verified in his reading of the Bible. Speaking of himself, he wrote:

> I know a man who affirms having experienced a number of times the torments of hell. This only lasted a short time, but the suffering was so great and so hellish that no language can express and no pen can describe it. [...] In these moments God appears as horribly irritated with him and even with the whole of creation. There is no escape possible, no consolation, neither in oneself or externally; there is nothing but accusation. And one sobs: "I am rejected far from thy face," not even daring to say: "Lord, in thine anger, do not condemn me." In such moments— this seems impossible—the soul cannot believe that such a prayer could ever be answered. It feels only that the punishment has not yet reached its full measure. And yet it is eternal ... (Lorz).

Ockhamism had explained that God was separated, that God was free of all determination and independent of any conceivable norm. No intrinsic consideration binds God, and concerning what is evil he can just as well decide that it is good, and vice versa. Ockhamism makes the sacraments mere external signs and goes so far as to affirm that God predestines some to heaven and others to hell by an arbitrary decree of his sovereignty (Ockham). The "Wholly Other" God that Luther finds in the Bible is far removed from all attributes of benevolent fatherhood.

What image of God did he find in the philosophy of his time, the only philosophy he knew? Ockhamism was not for him one philosophy among others; to his eyes it was philosophy. He rejects it, but it has already penetrated into his religious consciousness. Man's freedom, according to Ockham, is the power by which "I can indifferently and contingently produce an effect such that I may or may not cause it without the slightest difference resulting from the power itself" (Coppleston). The human will is free in relation to sensory inclination and even to the desire for happiness. If the will can refuse happiness, it is no longer possible to analyze the goodness of human actions in relation to an end that is necessarily desired. What gives direction to the will are the habits that it has taken on, but it can always react against habit and inclination; it remains free in principle.

This results in two moral alternatives, one theological and the other philosophical. According to the first, the free will is subject to obligation. God is free, but since man is entirely dependent, he is morally obliged to will what God commands him to will. According to St. Thomas, precepts were ordered according to natural law, which in turn was ordered according to what could be known of the divine essence, that is, divine law. But since it is now clear that we know nothing of this essence, moral law is based on a free divine choice. God can cause a bad action in the human will, but it ceases to be bad since it depends upon the divine *potentia abso-luta*. Hatred of God, rape and adultery are forbidden. But if God commanded them, they would become meritorious.

The other, purely philosophic moral teaching is based upon *recta ratio* or right reason. It is the approximative norm of morality. To accomplish what right reason prescribes is to desire what it prescribes because of this prescription. A human being can be mistaken in what he believes to be dictated by right reason. Thus it is always better to follow one's conscience, even if it is mistaken; "invincible ignorance" removes responsibility.

Ockham's moral teaching is therefore authoritarian: you must do it, because it is commanded by revelation or by reason. But you are capable of obeying, because your will is free. God (arbitrarily) grants indispensable grace, and even grants it unfailingly to the man who does what depends entirely on himself. It is not clear how this grace could be more than an ornament, a superfluity that crowns action. Here we are very close to Pelagianism.

Nothing here—except for the absolute transcendence of God, which here inclines toward the purely arbitrary—corresponded to Luther's intense experience. This "irreproachable monk," as he depicted himself, did everything that depended on himself. His nature inclined him to be extremely scrupulous. Yet his sin was always before his eyes and he feared hell. Few men have searched for justification by works to the degree Luther did. Luther lived in terror of God, stretched to the limit between divine demands and consciousness of sin. God appeared to him, as Cardinal Ratzinger observed, as the opposite of what he is: "a devil who wants to annihilate mankind."

But this ardent and pious Augustinian monk received no manifestation of grace. Luther was trying to grasp the state of grace experientially. "He wanted to know what was there, to feel it. For the future reformer, not to know whether one is in a state of grace and not to be in it is the same thing." (Lorz) in his notes on Tauler's sermons, he opposes *sapientia experimentalis* to *sapientia doctrinalis*. Simple, objective, receptive faith does not satisfy him. He always links the "grasping" of grace with election. When he feels nothing, he falls back into "temptation" and despair. Of course this process must be ascribed to Luther's individual character. It also has something to do with the education he received, not in this case his philosophical education, but the emotional, contemplative, sensory piety that was the expected fruit of the *devotion moderna*. In this Luther is a child of his age, completely removed from the syntheses of the thirteenth century. He rejects philosophy. He rejects the pursuit of meritorious works. He also rejects the humanism that Erasmus proposes to him. These three disciplines that gave form to the Christianity of his time were incapable of obtaining salvation, or even peace, in the soul of the monk Luther.

This is not the place to lay out Luther's radical solutions, such as: reason has no competence in the domain of faith; concupiscence is invincible and man always remains a sinner, impotent in regard to his own salvation of which God alone is the agent; Paul preached the radical opposition between the law and the gospel; salvation is given along with faith, and with certainty; God's anger is upon us but his mercy breaks forth in the Cross upon which Christ made himself a sinner, allowed the sins of men to be imputed to him, making men henceforth "at once sinners and justified." The point that interests us is that all these propositions rest upon the experience of the subject, on his subjectivity.

This can be understood, in the great tradition of Augustine and of the whole Church, as the attainment of a personal consciousness of religious life. Luther opposes the religion of personal inwardness, where the depths of the soul are engaged, to the religion of works. To receive the word as a grace and to accept it in faith as a salutary gift presupposes a personal decision, and the feeling that God is addressing a certain person, me, and not someone else. It suffices to read "On Christian Freedom" to understand that Luther's concern is to reestablish contact between the soul and Christ, to bring the soul back to an immediate and effective dependence on Christ. Thus he comments, in the little catechism, upon the second article of the Creed: "I believe that Jesus Christ [...] is my Lord, who has redeemed me and delivered me from all my sins, from death, and from slavery to the devil, I who was lost and damned, and has truly owned me and won me, not with silver or with gold, but with his precious blood and by his suffering and his innocent death, in order that I might belong entirely to him and that, living under his dominion, I might serve him in justice, perpetual innocence and felicity, just as he, who has risen from the dead, lives and reigns from age to age." There is no more orthodox confession of faith, nor one that is more Lutheran by its accent on the personal, and by its force and pathos. Luther writes "my Lord" and not "our Lord."

To liberate oneself from an obsessive fear of God becomes the unique problem of redemption. One attains this at the moment when faith appears as a deliverance from the personal claims of justice and as a personal certainty of salvation. Without this faith, without this certitude, there would be no redemption. Cardinal Ratzinger points out what here separates Luther from the Catholic faith: "thus we find here modified the mutual relationship among what are called the theological virtues of faith, hope and charity, the union of which may be considered as a sort of form of Christian existence: the certitude of hope and that of faith, which had been different in nature, become identical. For the Catholic, the certitude of faith rests on what God has done, of which the church bears to us the testimony. Certitude of hope refers to the salvation of individual persons and, among these, to my own Self. For Luther, however, this certitude constitutes precisely the central point apart from which nothing else counts. It is the reason for which charity, which for Catholics constitutes the interior form of faith, is entirely disassociated from the notion of faith." One thus ends up with the polemical formulations of the great commentary on the Epistle to the Galatians: *maledicta sit caritas*. The formula *sola fides,* on which Luther insists so much, signifies "this exclusion of charity from the problem of salvation." Charity is relegated to the domain of "works," works that are vain in relation to salvation. The *fides absoluta*, which is divine, is the cause of our justification. The *fides incarnate* does not concern justification as such, and this is why Luther could write: "*Loco charitatis justus ponimus fidem.*" In the place of charity we have put faith.

In a book of my youth, I had once observed that in Russian spirituality one finds at every step an opposition between the Father (the Pantocrator) and the kenotic, humiliated Christ. I had asked myself if there was not something Lutheran in this, without raising the question whether there had been some influence "which could only be from Germany to Russia" or whether this conception had been separately invented in the two countries, perhaps in relation to the respective political systems of Germany and Russia. In any case, we certainly find this dialectic in Luther's thought—perhaps pushed to the point of redoubling—in which, in an exclusive face-to-face between God and man, man must, against a God or a Christ who judges in anger, have recourse anew to a forgiving God. *Simul peccator et justus*: at once sinner and justified.

Luther thinks that the deliverance he brings is that which Christ had brought from the beginning of his preaching: "your sins are forgiven." Christianity, he writes, "is nothing but a permanent exercise on this point of doctrine, the feeling that you have no sins and that it is Christ who bears your sins." Max Weber, although a Lutheran, is of the view that the Catholic notion of sin followed by forgiveness (by the power of the Church), followed by a falling back into sin and then by forgiveness once again, an ongoing process, corresponds to the common experience of humanity, which Luther loses sight of. Luther's existential journey—anxiety-deliverance considered to be definitive—is given as a model, and it has in effect been the matrix of Lutheran humanity through the ages. His own subjectivity and his own spiritual experience have acquired the force of a norm for Christian life.

Lutheran Mysticism

It is obvious that Luther's quest is mystical in nature. Nevertheless he denies it, because he suspects mysticism of taking the place of the life of faith. Mysticism might reintroduce an emphasis on "works," on purely human efforts, which would be meritorious and tainted by Catholicism, into the relationship between God and the person of faith. Personal religion, which is the great ideal of the reformers, sees itself as threatened by the idea of a fusion of the soul with God, which would dissolve human personality in a vague and impersonal world. In the mind of the reformers

> the role of theology and the role of spirituality have been completely reversed. Spirituality, rather than being conceived as the blossoming of the life of faith, was conceived as it rule, and inversely theology, which was once the norm for this life of faith, was subjected to the experience of the spiritual life that it is reduced to describing. (Jaeger)

A contradiction thus arises between the desire to grasp God by experience and the impossibility of achieving such a grasp with certainty—for the *certidudo salutis* is a precarious state of consciousness, which can fall back into anxiety at any moment. The mystical temptation is opposed to justification by faith which absorbs all spiritual experience in the pure justification obtained by the imputation of Christ's merits. But this certainty remains personal, intimate, ineffable, incommunicable: "there is no use believing in the remission of sins if you do not believe, with absolute certainty, that your sins are remitted" (Jaeger)—for you individually, personally.

Jaeger has shown that, in Luther's spirituality, there is an encounter between negative mysticism, inherited from the Areopagite, which keeps Luther in darkness regarding God, and the mysticism inherited from Saint Bernard and from Tauler, which speaks of Christ crucified. For Luther Christ fills the void left by the theological life, which is "naked in his eyes." But he rejects the possibility of human vision going beyond to a contemplative state that would be fulfilled in union with the life of the Trinity. Such a passage beyond would be linked to the "theology of glory," considered to be incompatible with the "theology of the cross." Luther does not believe in the possibility of a continuity in spiritual life between the cross and glory. Glory is reserved to the other world; the cross cannot be transfigured.

The theology of the cross involves anxiety and cultivates spiritual travail. According to Luther, "every Christian must remain attached to the mystical cross." He refuses to take pleasure in some peaceful contemplation of divine things, which would amount to an "escape from the world." In its place, he offers an inner-worldly, severe and intransigent asceticism. One can see why so many Germans found Russia fascinating, for Russian spirituality somehow, by its strong sense of a Transfiguration that starts in this world and of the glorious Resurrection, enveloped the *theologia cruces* in a theology of glory, a sensibility that had nothing but disgust for the exhausting asceticism that it is horrified to find in German life.

The German Way after Luther

The positive affirmations of the Reformers—*sola fides, sola gratia, sola scriptura*—are not inimical to Catholic orthodoxy. What made them unacceptable was, as Louis Bouyer has said, the fact that the precious metals of doctrine were trapped in the gangue of nominalist philosophy, which neither the Reformers nor their Catholic adversaries were capable of criticizing. The Reformation might have reformed the whole Church, but it did not. Certain points of doctrine—forensic justification, grace not only free but incapable of transforming the person and instead leaving him *simul peccator et justus*, the certainty of salvation in faith—could not be accepted by the Catholic faith.

Doctrine is one thing, and the spiritual life of Reformed Christians is another. There is no doubt that, within both Lutheranism and Calvinism, no matter how hardened and shrunken doctrines had become in the writings and preaching of epigones, there were many holy lives, heroic in virtue to the point of martyrdom, which truly found in the Scriptures the nourishment they sought. Such lives, by their manifest holiness, give us cause to doubt this doctrine of grace that leaves the forensically justified believer in a state of sin.

On the one hand, the systematic thinkers of Lutheranism and Calvinism have, over the centuries, proposed several orthodoxies and neo-orthodoxies. These theologies and these theologians have had their hour of glory, but there is not one among them whose reputation has not declined with the passage of time, and none has been able to rally Protestantism as a whole around him in a lasting way, nor even the Lutheran, Calvinist, Baptist and other subgroups. The dominant authority of Karl Barth, whom Pope Paul VI considered the greatest theologian of his time, declined rapidly after his death.

On the other hand, among the faithful, the positive principles of the Reformation demonstrate their fecundity: salvation by faith, by grace alone, personal religion, the living meaning of Scripture, and the glory of God. Periodically, this individual religion becomes contagious, warms up collectively, and we witness an Awakening, which can last for years. During these awakenings, the positive principles take hold naturally. The divisions among Christians seem to disappear in the warmth of communal piety, but only as long as these divisions are not stimulated by the spirit of controversy. Still, these forms of religious life, both individual and collective, are essentially subjective, since they are based on lived experience. Not only do they involve emotion, but this emotion becomes the sign and even the proof of the authenticity of Christian life. Emotion is sought for its own sake.

In the seventeenth century, Lutheranism in Germany settles into a new form. It returns to an orthodoxy that is substantially Catholic, but without the name. An abundant literature of spirituality draws from patristic authors and from the medieval mystics. Arndt produces guides to the inner life that won him the name of the Thomas à Kempis of the Protestant world. His disciple Gerhardt continues this work, a new *Imitatio Christi*. The authors of the *devotion moderna*, Tauler and St. Bernard, together with Luther's *Little Catechism*, inspire a doctrine of a union with Christ that penetrates the whole of existence: "It is faith that shapes the love of Christ in the faithful heart."

Faith in Protestant lands lies in hearing. *Fides ex auditu.* "Ears are the only organs of a Christian," Luther said. The Word is put to music. Pure music is as penetrating a message as the word spoken or sung. It works upon the soul, bringing the mystery to life. It intensifies the word, and intensity is a feature of the Protestant soul, because it better expresses the experience of the faith. Music takes the place occupied by methodical visual contemplation in the Catholic soul, for example in Saint Ignatius's *Exercises*, or the icon for the Orthodox soul. In its ineffability, it accords with a hidden and distant God and with Lutheran negative theology. The choir, Luther's great liturgical innovation, is further enriched by the hymns and poems of Paul Gerhardt. The transcendent purity of Bach's music expresses the objective character that Luther accords to justification by faith alone.

The "Formula of Concord" (1580) had defined the essentials of Lutheran doctrine. The power to organize the Churches had been assumed by the princes and, unsurprisingly, Lutheran orthodoxy took on features of sterility, of authoritarian bureaucratization. Then, in 1675, the *Pia Desideria* of Jacob Spener appeared, which was the birth of the vast and enduring movement we call pietism. Pietism affirms that a living faith engenders a piety that manifests itself in visible fruits, the first of which is love. There is thus a slippage from forensic justification to an experienced sanctification, visible in life and—in the eyes of the severe guardians of orthodoxy—in works. The "pious desires" are six in number: to constitute circles of piety, private meetings devoted to the study of Scripture and to mutual edification; to bring lay members and pastors together, according to the universal priesthood of the baptized; to add to the knowledge of doctrine the practice of the virtues; to show love in controversy, and to renounce in particular all hateful disputes; to develop in students a concern for salvation just as lively as their zeal for their studies; and, finally, to renew preaching by having it emphasize the new man. Spener's fame spread, as he was called successively to Dresden and then finally to Berlin, as the first pastor of Saint-Nicolas church. Despite attacks against him (the theology faculty at Wittenberg attributed to him three hundred heretical or erroneous opinions), but sustained by a contemporaneous wave of Illuminism throughout Germany, he was able to found a faculty of theology in the new university of Halle, which became a major center for the spread of pietism in all of central Europe and as far as Russia. The little circles of intellectuals that were formed in Russia and all over Europe in the nineteenth century originated partly in circles of Baptist piety.

The second Baptist generation is dominated by the strong personality of August Hermann Francke. He oversaw the instruction in Halle of thousands of pastors, who were sent to him by the Prussian king. The movement spread out over the Low Countries, Scandinavia, England—and thereby to America—and even to Russia. But after his death the Pietist movement descended into simplistic sentimentalism. It became concentrated in Württemberg, where it sank deep roots. We will have occasion further on to say more concerning Bengel and Öttinger, who sprang from this milieu.

Count Zinzendorf (1700–1760) revived pietism in its third generation. Formed in Francke's *pedagogium* as a student in Halle, he was an ardent religious soul who dreamed of founding a religious order that would transform the world. Already as an eight-year-old child he experienced ecstatic impulses that contained the germ of what he would later call his "theology of the heart." He experienced several exceptional mystical states. Traveling in Europe as required by his high birth, he would encounter pious Calvinist circles in the Low Countries. In France he became acquainted with

Cardinal Noailles, a somewhat confused prelate, and with his entourage, which made a big impression on him. "They descended with me into the unsearchable depths of the passion and of the merits of Christ, and of the grace acquired at this price, of joy and of holiness. Thus we dwelt together in intimacy, the heart full of a celestial joy, and we worried no more concerning what might be exactly the religion of one or the other" (Gusdorf). He returned to Germany convinced that the "theology of the heart" could unite all sincere Christians. He conceived the Church as an ecumenical utopia of unity, where Lutherans and Calvinists might unite with Catholics, each retaining its particular theological convictions, differences reconciled yet not effaced (Bouyer). On his seigneurial lands he organized a community that attracted Moravians, who belonged to the tradition of the Bohemian Brethren of the Bishop Comenius, established in the previous century. The Moravian Brethren lived in a kind of familial monastery. Marriages were made only with the consent of the elected leaders of the community. Children were raised outside their families in two boarding schools. Life was organized around a daily schedule of services, in which the "brothers" and the "sisters" took turns so that collective prayer was uninterrupted.

Then there were some troubles with the Halle pietists. They reproached him in particular for failing to practice what Francke called the *agône penitentiae*, that is, a deep conviction of sin which is then suddenly wiped away by grace. Zinzendorf tried, but found in himself only a "spiritual convulsion" of those suffered by children who are teething.

Before leaving Saxony, he threw himself into missionary expeditions in Greenland, in Georgia, and in Livonia. After the English parliament officially recognized his Church under the name of the *Unitas Fratrum* or United Brethren, he settled in London. His personal theology began to go beyond the limits of extravagance. The influence of ideas of Boehme and Arnold is visible, but his thought is mainly the expression of an increasingly sentimentalist tendency. One finds a constant evocation of the Savior's pierced side and of the flowing blood in which those born again by grace must delight in bathing themselves. We are close here to a Protestant *kitsch* that rivals the Catholic *kitsch* of the late nineteenth century.

How should one assess this vast and multi-faceted movement called pietism? It shares certain features with what in the Calvinist world are called Awakenings, yet it is a notably less massive and popular phenomenon. It is also less visible, insofar as the tradition of inward faith and of the invisibility of the Church are well established in German lands. And it is important to take into account the political structure, which is still that of the old regime, under which the power of the princes to whom Luther had left the control of Churches is still in effect. The large camp meetings seen in America and in Wales are unimaginable in these principalities; they would be impossible and forbidden.

Still, this movement shares with the Awakenings an affective and simplified style of religion. This affectivity is oriented toward love—familial love, love of neighbor, love in principle among Christians of different confessions. There is the same aspiration to virtue and practice of mutual exhortation in the warm, even burning enclosure of the *collegium pietatis* as one finds in the separatist congregations.

Despite vaguely ecumenical notions, there is no question of a return to Catholicism. The borders are sealed, and no one passes. On the other hand, there is a powerful attraction to set forms of Christian life, and most clearly to the *devotion moderna*. Similarities include peaceful inner devotion, delight in the nourishment of the Scriptures, especially the Gospels and Paul's Letters, practiced in silence in the home, within a family united in prayer. Along with favorite authors such as Saint Bernard, *The Imitation*, Tauler, and Ruysbroeck, there are also modern authors, sometimes even Catholic ones, such as Francis of Sales, Fenelon, and Madame Guyon. This is a touching portrait that moves the hardened French of the Enlightenment, sensitive as they are to this sweet and good Germany submissive to its authorities, zealous each within the condition where he has been placed, but with a deep foundation of tranquil joy based on the certainty of salvation, a rich inner life and a delicate culture of religious feeling. On the one hand, the pietistic awakening recovers one of the richest deposits of Christianity, along with medieval authors; on the other, it runs the permanent risk of lapsing into a formless and complacent sentimentalism.

Schleiermacher

This latter aspect had its theoretician. Frederic Schleiermacher was born in Breslau in 1768. He belonged to the Reformed Church, but he was above all a child of pietism. He was acquainted with the Moravian Brotherhood and shared with them the piety of the conventicle, the preoccupation with the fall and with corruption, and the duty of an ascetic life. Named pastor in Berlin, and having fallen in love platonically and unhappily with a colleague's wife, he was obliged to withdraw for two years until 1804, still a pastor, to a little town. Nevertheless, his stay in Berlin put him in contact with F. Schlegel, and through him with all the great philosophical minds, such as Schelling, Fichte, and Novalis. Then he began a university career, returned to Berlin, and was named professor of theology from the university's founding in 1810, a function that he filled until his death in 1834.

Here then is a man who was parish pastor for ten years, responsible for a community of the faithful, and who nevertheless in his writings affirmed that he believed neither in a transcendent creator God, nor in the divinity of Jesus Christ, nor in any of the symbols of the Christian faith. Yes he saw no contradiction between his convictions and his office. What then did he preach throughout his life (in ten published volumes) with ardor, with enthusiasm, and with communicative effusion? What he preached was neither Christianity, nor reformed Christianity; he preached *religion*.

What is religion? He explains this to us in his youthful work which appeared in 1799, the main theses of which he never denied, and which are still famous: *Discourse on Religion: Speeches to its Cultured Despisers*.

He demonstrates that the supreme and necessary complement to human life, beyond the sciences and the arts, is the direct worship of the Absolute, the Infinite, the Divine, of "God," which he prefers to designate by the name Universe. "Religion was the maternal bosom in whose obscurity my youth was nourished … it was still there for me when God and the immortality of the soul disappeared from my vision, dismissed by doubt." One must thus imagine something like a Kantian type of religion, but one from which God and the immortality of the soul have been removed. Lichtenberg, his contemporary, might well have found here a new application of the "knife without a blade which is missing the handle."

In the somewhat exalted style of German romanticism, still warmed by "religion," Schleiermacher declares that he addresses neither the English, miserable positivists and empiricists, nor the French, incurably light-minded and frivolous, but serious Germans. He reproaches idealism for reducing the world to a "simple allegory, a reflection of our own very limited spirit without real existence." To this he opposes the superior realism of Spinoza, "for whom the Infinite was the alpha and the omega, and the Universe the object of his sole and eternal love." Religion adds to metaphysics the direct sentiment of this Infinite, toward which philosophy tends without being able to attain it. Concerning morality and its relation to religion, he writes: "Every activity in the proper sense must and can be moral, but religious feelings must accompany everything man does as a sacred music. He must do everything with religion, nothing by religion."

But just what is religion? "In its essence religion is neither thought nor action, it is intuition and feeling. It wishes intuitively to grasp the Universe [i.e., God], to watch him piously in his manifestations and his actions, to open oneself to his penetrating influence in a childlike passivity." This intuition is a fusion of the subject and the object. Schleiermacher recommends that those who aspire to immortality extinguish their individuality already in this world in order to live in the One and the All. This is obviously a theme resonant with Plotinus, filtered through Eckhart and Boehme. This fusion, which may only last an instant, is the "moment of birth" of all that is living in religion. This new birth is what renders faith and the rules of conduct communicated and dictated by the tradition truly religious, by informing them with a personal life.

Separated from the gangue of romanticism, this is the fundamental idea of the Baptists.

Dogmas are the abstract expression of religious intuitions, and this is their only value. And revelation? Every original and new intuition of the Universe is a revelation. Grace? All religious feelings are supernatural, and faith is enlivened and living only by feelings. Scripture? "The Holy Scriptures became the Bible by their own intrinsic power, but they do not forbid any other book to be or to become a Bible, and the Scriptures would willingly be added to by whatever might be written of equal power."

All religions have their *raison d'être*—natural religions, Eastern religions, Judaism (he says not a word concerning Islam), and the various Christian confessions. All are imperfect. But all share the same aspiration to the Infinite (another name of God). The historical Christ responded to this aspiration. What is divine in him is the great clarity by which he attained in his soul, the great idea that he came in order to represent (Schleiermacher avoids saying "incarnate"), the idea that every finite being needs "superior mediations" in order to be connected with Divinity. To be sure, he is not the only mediator; he must content himself with being the "mediator par excellence." And sin? The word is never pronounced. In its place we find expressions such as "estrangement from the Universe," "irreligion," or "evil."

In a later work, *The Christian Faith According to the Principles of the Evangelical Faith*, published in 1821, but without retracting anything from the *Discourse*, Schleiermacher returns to the theme of intuition, which he henceforth calls "the feeling of piety." This is a feeling of dependence or of a relationship with God, which is known by all religions. What is the reference of this feeling? Where does it come from? Well, this feeling is precisely what we call God, and it is sufficient proof of his existence. We know nothing of the origins of sin and of evil. The story of the Fall has been dismissed, and with it the notion of a fall. But the fact remains that we are estranged from God, which we are aware of through the opposition between the flesh and the spirit, between man and God. Christ, who is not subject to this opposition, is a model by which human beings can find guidance in order to return to God, and, after death, to enjoy, not immortality, but the feeling of being transported beyond time, a feeling he will already have experienced fleetingly in his terrestrial existence when he felt himself in full communion with the Absolute. Paradise and hell are notions unworthy of religion.

Liberalism

We have perhaps said enough to give a simplified but not inaccurate idea of Schleiermacher's theology. What is interesting is that he was hailed in Germany as a "second Luther" and as towering figure who dominated religious thought until the twentieth century. He was received as a liberator, after two centuries of state administration of the Church and of desiccated orthodoxy. Strauss and Bauer followed in his footsteps, though they saw themselves as historians rather than as theologians. Albert Ritschl, professor in Bonn and later Göttingen, a disciple of Bauer as well as of Kant, held that the goal of religion was not to offer superior knowledge, but to provide a "life ideal" and to allow the Christian to hold to standards of ethical behavior proper to the attainment of the kingdom of God. This kingdom comes into being to the degree that the Christian seeks in love the moral reorganization of humanity. This synthesis between Christianity and culture was a good fit for Wilhelmian Germany. It should be noted that this *Kulturprotestantismus* adamantly blames pietism for importing Catholic elements into Protestant faith. With some good reason, it defines pietism as "a crypto-Catholic, mystical movement of piety, inimical to the world." (Cornuz)

Still, the greatest authority of liberal Protestantism was Harnack. He was above all a great historian. In theology he thought that Christianity had gone through four steps: Jewish, Greek, Roman and now Germanic. This was a continuous process, because the message had gradually settled out and been purified. This is why he so admired Marcion, to whom he devoted a book of magnificent erudition, because he was one of those who, before Luther, with whom he compares him, had separated the spirit from the letter in which it was enclosed. In the last of the lectures held before the faculties of the University of Berlin, published under the title *The Essence of Christianity*, he concludes in this way:

> Jesus opens for us the perspectives of a human society in which cohesion will not be a matter of legal constraint, but where love will reign and the enemy will be conquered by mildness. What a noble and sublime ideal we have received in this, from the foundation of our religion, an ideal that must remain the goal and the north star of all historical development. Will humanity ever attain it? Who can say? But we can and we must approach it, and we are beginning today to feel, very differently from two or three centuries ago, that for us it is a moral obligation to march in this direction.

We marched in this direction toward the Great War and the twentieth century.

Such an argument might have been made by thinkers who owed nothing to Protestantism or even to Christianity. A progressive spiritualization of civilization, with a kindly regard for the Christian origins from which one is pleased to be emancipated—all this is consonant with any number of nineteenth-century philosophers. Someone like Renan, for example, would not have disagreed. Protestant liberalism tends to merge with the spiritualism that enjoys such prestige at the end of this century. Bergson gives a definition of intuition which, though it probably owes nothing to Schleiermacher, could have been ratified by him.

But let us return to the author who is crucial to this evolution, that is, to Schleiermacher. He was not only well-informed philosophically, but himself a capable philosopher, and his dealings with Schelling were between equals. But where religion was concerned, he radically evacuated philosophical thought and wished to have no foundation but feeling. He brings to completion an evolution of Lutheranism begun three centuries earlier. Luther had put his own spiritual experience, his own personal drama and the solution he had found, at the center of the Reformation. But behind this experience the whole system of Christian faith subsisted, constructed one stone upon another, over sixteen centuries. Thus, even if he rejected a few stones, the essence of the building remained substantially intact. Luther refers to Augustine, to the Church Fathers, and even to the scholastic theology of his day, which he rejects but upon which he remains dependent. Then, behind the screen of Lutheran orthodoxy, which is based on inner experience, and the purely psychological feeling of faith, the dogmatic structure little by little evaporated. A bifurcation arose. On the one hand there is the Bible, the piety that is nourished by it, inward meditation, the impulses of conscience, and on the other hand there is philosophy. For, far from dying in Lutheran lands, philosophy continues and flourishes. It separates itself slowly from the theosophy that had constituted, with Eckhart and Boehme, its initial soil. In the eighteenth century, Bengel, Öttinger and Swedenborg build their systems of nature and of history, which by no means break with religion, but on the contrary descend into the depths of apocalyptic mysticism. Kant, on the contrary, rejects what he considers a hodgepodge. Detached from dogmas from the outset, he seeks to reconstruct what can be saved "within the limits of reason." Then the great idealist line takes off, presenting itself, in the case of Hegel, as a great quasignostic reinterpretation of all of Christianity, but in such a way that he is able to declare himself unequivocally Lutheran.

Hasso Jaeger sees the rise of German philosophy as a consequence of the extreme demands that Lutheranism imposes on the faithful, who must bear the "mystical cross" of justification, a drama that produces in the soul a permanent tension between perdition and salvation. The person, diminished in his ontological substance, now really exists as a person only in the very act of justification. What results is spiritually exhausting. The risk thus emerges of looking for relief from the burden of the personal cross by adhering to a system that offers instead a tragic universal fatalism whose principle is grounded in the world and in history. In the twentieth century, however, this grandiose gnosis sheds its religious elements.

Following Hegel, but already in his day, German philosophy takes up in its own way the irreligion, even the avowed atheism of the French and English Enlightenment. This is the time of Schopenhauer, of Feuerbach, of the Left Hegelians, of Marx and subsequent scientism, and then of the ideologies of the twentieth century. Nevertheless, alongside all this, "religion" continues on its way, but more and more meager and thin. It is as if sentimentalism, having evacuated the consideration of the scientific and philosophic world, also evacuated dogma. All Christian dogmas, not to mention properly Lutheran dogmas, have disappeared in Schleiermacher's liberalism.

Still, we must not take Schleiermacher's personal religion as a standard and measure of the real state of Christianity in its Lutheran version. Apart from all speculative ambition, in popular piety, in enlightened piety, as well as in souls that aspire to perfection, there exists a Christian life that is by no means drying up. It draws upon the same sources that have always served it well during theologically impoverished periods or when systematic thought has little to offer: the Bible, of course, and the familiar authors of the *devotion moderna*, and spiritual thinkers such as Arndt, Tersteegen, and Spener, who continue this tradition. Finally, faith is strengthened by the significant manifestation of Christian orthodoxy found in the Lutheran choral liturgy and in great music.

An Average Protestantism: Zwingli

As with every revolutionary process, the revolution initiated by Luther produced a "left" and a "right." The left interpreted the Reformation as liberating anarchy in the Church and in the State, and it revived the apocalyptic evangelism that had never wholly disappeared since the thirteenth century. These were the first bloody steps of Anabaptism that the lords crushed with Luther's wrathful approval. The Baptist movement would survive, as we shall see.

But on the right it was no longer a matter of sects of the medieval kind, but of respectably bourgeois churches that quickly developed in Switzerland and in the string of prosperous cities of the Rhine valley. Zwingli represents this movement more than he invents it. This reasonable Protestantism is supported by the authorities, especially by the Hohenzollern of Prussia, because it is easy to govern. The Zwinglian state of mind is located at the end of a process that started in the cooling of Lutheran and Calvinist piety. Here a peaceful and lukewarm equilibrium is reached. Hard Calvinism, after evacuating Switzerland and the German Rhineland, will endure only in Holland and in Scotland, among the English dissidents – and then in America.

Doctrines are fluid. One can see the radicalization of "evangelical" tendencies that prepared the Reformation, but without going so far, the master of which was Erasmus, who found partisans in France such as Rabelais, Lefèvre d'Étaples, and Cisneros or Carranza in Spain and More or Pole in England. This is a humanism in love with reason, and which draws on the Platonist side of Augustine. When it commits to the Reformation and breaks with traditional dogma, this humanism still retains something, by atavism or by conservatism. This is once again the spirit of the *devotio moderna*, but partially shorn of the supernatural, and more completely in the next generation in thinkers such as Castellion, Servetus, and Socinus, all precursors of all later forms of "Unitarianism." Zwingli still voices the dogmas of the Trinity, of Incarnation and of Redemption, and even some Marian doctrines (perpetual virginity). But these are no longer axes of the faith. The Gospels, or rather the evangelical soul, are the whole of religion. Justification by faith is certainly professed, but it is equivalent to a simple justification by inward piety toward Christ. Religious institutions are no longer of value. The sacraments no longer hold any mystery. They are images for simple people that remind us what is taught to us by the Word alone, the love of God in Jesus Christ (Bouyer). Aggression against the Catholic Eucharist is spectacular. The emblems are henceforth distributed four times a year, with a dish and a wooden cup, on an ordinary table, and received standing by the communicants arranged in a circle. It is only a memorial that has nothing to do with the presence of Christ. And this Christ, according to a plainly Nestorian conception, seems much like a man who is exceptionally conscious of the presence of God in him. Original Sin is reduced to a kind of moral sickness which the Redeemer, as a religious psychologist, comes to heal in human beings and, by his example, to guide them toward the life of the children of God.

We find already in Zwinglianism, still expressed with sixteenth-century vigor, the themes that will come out again in the most extenuated pietism, particularly the constantly repeated opposition between the inward and the outward. The outward (sacraments, church institutions, ascetic practices) is either the expression of the inward, or else an idolatrous superstition. Plato and a platonic Augustine have imprinted in this religiosity the idea that man is spirit, that is, a soul foreign to matter that receives nothing from it but corruption.

Such a spirituality, the product of a weathered Lutheranism and of a platonic humanism, is already a "religion within the limits of reason." It is also a piety with no defined relation to dogma, concerning which it feels free and which it can cast off without effort or pain. Tillich is in this tradition when he affirms that the Protestant principle is the rejection of all mediation between God and man. Does he go beyond this tradition when he adds that this God is only the symbol of his best and deepest self? The answer is not clear.

Zwingli's humanistic Reformation is elitist. It shares the detestation of cultivated circles for the superstitions of popular piety and for the nonsense that piles up in the churches. Once his friends are masters of the state, Zwingli forcibly imposes the suppression of pilgrimages, of processions, and of images. The housecleaning was over in thirteen days: the painting over of frescoes and the removal or destruction of statues and paintings (Chaunu). Like all the reformers, and also according to the medieval conception, he confuses Christendom with the social body. He suggests a kind of proto-democratic constitution and justifies the sacraments of baptism and of the Last Supper as the festivals of a society demonstrating that it is imbued with the gospel. The urban aristocracy did not follow it on this terrain. The free cities and the little churches appreciated the emancipation from the Church, but they were not about to be governed by preachers. The faithful masses followed this Reformation with satisfaction, continued to practice the sacraments because they are in the gospel, but, as they became more and more educated, considered them increasingly to be an embarrassing remainder, a lesson in images with which one can eventually dispense.

Calvin's Theology

The Reformation was an accident that happened within a general wave of fervor and because of this same fervor. Luther's insurrection was not at first directed against the vices and defects of the Roman church, but against its impiety, its loss of a sense of God, of His Majesty and transcendence, the insult He was exposed to every day by unworthy practices believed to bring salvation. The whole of Western Europe, both lands that remained Catholic and those that became Protestant, was moved by the same religious enthusiasm; the Reformed areas were the most intense.

But already in Luther's later years this tremendous movement began to decline. The humanist reform in the free cities of the Rhine and the little states of the Helvetic zone invented very early what would later become the tepid formula of liberal Protestantism: "free thought merely colored with mystical moralism" (Bouyer).

This is why Calvin should be seen in the same perspective as Karl Barth. Both react with the same haughty vigor to the blandness, this time not of Protestantism but simply of Christianity, whose biblical purity they aim to restore. Neither can be understood without adopting the elevated point of view of a mysticism so high, so austere, and so modest that it wishes not to be seen as such, for fear of falling back into the idolatry and the magic that it believes afflicts Catholic mysticism.

There is a word that appears over and over again in Calvin's treatises and sermons: *idolatry*. Man's incorrigible tendency is to be "a storehouse of idols." Before Christianity, but also under Christianity, man manages to put the creature on the level of the

Creator. With extraordinary force, Calvin restores the figure of the God of the Bible and of the prophets, the sovereign Being from whom all reality proceeds and who cannot be anything other than himself. This is the sense of the glory of God that characterizes the creature before the fall as well as the creature restored in Christ. This creature attributes to him and to him alone the source and the reality of all that is good, that is, glory. *Soli Deo Gloria.* In Christ, the hidden God reveals himself, but he does so as hidden and remains, as St. Paul said, "in inaccessible light," escaping our highest thoughts and our most grandiose speculations. The meaning of Calvinist mysticism, as well as Calvinism's distrust for mysticism, in which he always sees a risk of idolatry, lies in this intuition of God as the Sovereign, the Holy, the Wholly Other, such that Calvin discourages in advance any idea of representation (hence Calvin's decided iconoclasm), even verbal. In an offshoot of Calvinism, among the disciples of George Fox, and among the Quakers, these principles are pushed to the extreme. There are still signs of the nakedness of the Calvinist Temple and of its stripped-down form of worship. The Quakers no longer have a temple, ritual worship, or even ritual prayer, and the only praise that they find appropriate and worthy of an absolutely transcendent God is, finally, silence. As Maimonides said: "for thee silence is praise." Calvin made an exception for the Psalms but would tolerate no other reading in the liturgy.

This Calvinist mysticism—which St. John of the Cross in Catholic Spain knows and formulates in very similar terms—makes it possible to situate correctly the doctrine of the sacraments and the famous question of predestination.

On the question of the Eucharist Calvin seems to distance himself from Luther, who believed in the real presence in the holy species, and to approach the views of Zwingli, who saw there nothing but a symbolic memorial without real content. He rejects the Catholic affirmation of transubstantiation as well as the Lutheran faith in a presence *in, cum, sub pane.* The body of Christ is in heaven (Gagnebin), and there is no question of having it come down into an earthly element nor of breaking it up on the altars.

But by the indubitable word that offers to us the body and the blood of Christ, we ourselves are lifted up to this heaven where he dwells and we are nourished spiritually from his body. Calvin thus builds a mysticism of union of the Christian with Christ and of incorporation by his resurrected being. He makes this the basis of his ecclesiology.

Nevertheless Calvin cannot admit, any more than Luther, a real conjunction between the Creator and his creature. We remain in a *forensic* perspective. The refusal of an objective presence therefore leaves separated on the one hand the bread, which remains bread, and on the other the believer, who is only in heaven through feeling, an emotion produced in him by the word that he accepts in faith. Instead of attaining its object, faith maintains itself by the sight of the sign and the hearing of the word, and so there is no avoiding a return to a Zwinglian sacrament, a purely mental evocation of the object of faith (Bouyer).

In 1562 Calvin preaches a sermon on the Epistle to the Ephesians (Gagnebin). "If one asks why God has pity on one party and why he leaves behind another, there is no answer except that it so pleases him [...]. We will never know whence proceeds our salvation until we have lifted our senses up to this eternal counsel of God by which he chose those he wished to choose, leaving the others in their confusion and their ruin." The unknown god of the Bible here merges with the Ockham's unknowable God. *De potentia Dei absoluta*, good and evil are interchangeable, salvation and perdition, according to his good pleasure. Yet, at the same time, Christian salvation and the certitude of this salvation must be established on a basis that our own fragility cannot compromise. And there is no other security than the will of God, such as it is fulfilled in His sovereign freedom. It is when man renders to God alone the glory that, far from feeling crushed by this, he finds an assurance of true peace and of true joy. "Our presumption is too enormous when we wish to impose a law upon God, such that it is only permissible for him to do what we conceive and what to us seems just. It is therefore a matter of worshiping God's secrets, which are incomprehensible for us."

"There are two main things we must strive for and it is even the sum of everything God teaches us by Holy Scripture and the point of all our studies and of our senses. One is that God be magnified as he deserves; the second is that we be certified for our salvation." Calvin finds the idea of election in the Old Testament: why did God choose Abraham and his household, and not another people? And in the New Testament: why have we received the grace to have the gospel preached us and to discern it by the grace of the Holy Spirit? Here is the basis of the "'assurance of our salvation.' To pray to God we must call him our Father, even if we are pupils of our Lord Jesus Christ, because he has shown us this. [...] But in order to 'pray well we must have faith in Jesus Christ who has pledged us this.'"

"When God wished to love us, that he cast an eye upon us 'in no way, for he would have found us detestable.'" He loved us in Jesus Christ, who is the "mirror in which he contemplates us." Scripture calls God's election *the book of life*. Jesus Christ "serves as a register; it is in him that we are engraved and that God recognizes us as his children."

The faithful, torn away from the perversion of doctrines and the un-Christlike domination of the papist church, sure of their faith and persevering in the confidence that results from true faith, had no doubt that they belong, as Weber says, "to the limited aristocracy of salvation" (Crouzet). Quite contrary to what is imagined in Catholic countries, predestination, far from causing anxiety, is a source of peace, of assurance, of joy. The Calvinist has put himself in God's hands once and for all. "If God's providence shines in the heart of the faithful not only will he be delivered from the fear and distress that once pressed upon him, but he will be relieved of all doubt. For, just as we are right to fear fortune, so we have good reason to dare boldly to put ourselves in God's hands. It is thus a great relief for us to hear that the Lord holds all things in his power, that he governs by his will and moderates by his patience such that nothing comes about that he has not intended" (Gagnebin). The caprices of Fortune become events willed by God, and they cease to frighten us.

The certainty of belonging to the flock of saints, to the aristocracy of salvation, will soon be colored in Calvinist lands by a feeling of social aristocracy. There is a congenital link between the circles in which Calvinism prospered and the urban patriciate, first in the cities of the Rhine, and then on the American East Coast. This social success is ascribed by the Calvinist conscience to the doctrine of sanctification.

The doctrine of sanctification is the fundamental contribution of Calvin to Protestantism in general. Luther placed the cause of salvation in God alone. Justification by faith did not go beyond itself. It embraced everything and was sufficient to itself. Afterwards it was up to man to organize his life.

There was in this teaching the possibility of subjectivism. To the *sola fide, sola gratia* Calvin added the *soli Deo gloria*. This means that God is not only in the cause and in the means, he is also in the end. The creative act does not stop in man, but must return to God: "How can God come into our thoughts, except that at the same time we think that, since we are his workmanship, and by right of nature and creation we are subject to his power, that our life belongs to him, that everything we undertake and do must be referred to him?" (Bouyer) And further on: "the duty of the faithful is to offer their body to God as a living host, holy and pleasing. [...] We are consecrated and dedicated to God in order no longer to think, speak, meditate or do anything except to his glory [...]. We do not belong to ourselves: let us therefore forget ourselves as much as possible, and everything that surrounds us. Thus we are the Lord's: let us live and die with him. We are the Lord's: let his will and his wisdom therefore preside in all of our actions. We are the Lord's; let every part of our life be referred to him." Faith does not suffice. It is authentic and salutary only if it leads to a sanctification of the whole being.

Calvin seems to return to the traditional doctrine: a faith that does not produce a progressive sanctification is only the appearance of faith and produces no justification. But this is not quite so. It is indeed the Holy Spirit who guides this new life, but his only gift seems to be that of the understanding of Scripture. Scripture is perfectly clear and without mystery. Calvin, like the other reformers, ignores history as development. This means that he does not see the creative evolution between the Old and the New Testament and that the law of Christ is reducible to a correct discernment of the requirements of the Decalogue (Bouyer). Like Luther, he refuses truly to locate the effects of grace within the faithful. The gifts of God remain external: this is still *forensic* grace. The glory of God is not communicated to man, as if God could not be great without man's remaining pure nothingness. He would not say of this jealous God (of a very human jealousy), as did St. Irenaeus, that his true glory is the living human being. As strange as the comparison may appear, the idea of an arbitrary and unpredictable God, *de potentia absoluta*, combined with the idea of the divine law given all at once to man who must obey—one cannot help but think sometimes of Islam.

The Life of Sanctification

At least Calvin is much clearer than Luther in providing a program for life. He describes it in detail in *The Institutes of the Christian Religion* and his sermons. The life of sanctification is a life of work, of the reasonable enjoyment of goods, and of mortification.

Work is a curse that by the fall was made a part of the human species (Gagnebin). But if work is now imposed by force, it is also a part of our nature. Was not Adam, before sinning, "put in the garden to cultivate it"? Already then it was necessary that human beings take part in some labor, to which "we must apply ourselves all through our lives." The blessing of God "will be on the hands of those who work." Therefore let each know his vocation and follow it. "Let every person and his place esteem that his state is like a station assigned by God so that he might not flutter about and turn here and there thoughtlessly for the rest of his life." But this work must be guided by God. The man who works presents to God "the offering of his hands to say: 'Lord it pleases you that I work; well then! Off I go, but I know that there will be no profit in it unless you guide me, unless you give me a good result.'"

Calvin is moderate concerning asceticism. He does not want it to deprive us unreasonably of the legitimate fruits of divine benevolence, nor that it brutalize man and render him "like a block of wood." The target is the monastic asceticism of the papists. "Let us learn also to bear poverty patiently and with a peaceful heart, and to make use of abundance moderately." Let the rich put aside "superfluity" and let the poor learn patiently to do without what they lack. One must "learn to be rich" in such a way as to moderate greed and to be rich with decency. For all things, though they may belong to us truly and legitimately, are given to us by the kindness of God and destined to our utility, and "they are like an account that we will someday have to answer for." Let men clothe themselves "neatly," nothing more, and let women be modest and humble in their apparel. As St. Peter said, "our ornament is internal." Finally there is mortification: "we can say that the life of a Christian is a study and a perpetual exercise in the mortification of the flesh until, this flesh being deadened, the Spirit of God reigns in us. Thus I hold that he who has learned to go against his own pleasure in many things has much benefited; not that he stop at this point and go no further, but rather in order that he sigh and long for God and that, being planted in the death and resurrection of Christ, he make it his study to observe continual penitence."

The way of life imposed by sanctification cannot remain an individual preference. Church and state have a stake in it. Before taking up this matter, I wish to include a digression.

Anxiety and Its Remedies

Anxiety is for all times and all people. The oldest texts testify to it. There is reason to think it is more present or more acute in certain areas or certain civilizations. I do not know of a place where it would be as conscious and poignant as in Western Europe. One might even wonder whether the world of Latin Christianity does not love anxiety. For better or for worse, anxiety accompanies its dynamism and is probably one of its essential factors. The master of the West, Augustine, left behind certain theological teachings that encourage its cultivation. By drawing from the ancient world and the Greek Church Fathers, the Thomist school worked toward an equilibrium in which this dark cloud would not take up such a big place on the horizon. The point of equilibrium, albeit relative, that was attained in the thirteenth century breaks down and unleashes anxiety in the two subsequent centuries, centuries of catastrophes, uncertainties, the plague, war, and the division of the Church. These are also the centuries of rapid progress of the individualism that allows the personal expression of anxiety.

Lutheranism is the narration of an unbearable crisis of anxiety and of the sudden relief from it found in the reception of the saving gift of faith. But anxiety always returns. The remedy is thus to renew the act of faith. And what if it returns again? A kind of alternation arises between anxiety and faith, and finally a confusion. Spiritual torment becomes a criterion of the authenticity of faith. Henceforth anxiety is cultivated; it goes along with piety. The person, radically corrupted by sin and without his own ontological consistency, is as it were obliterated in the event of justification and replaced, *forensically*, by Christ as Savior, "Christ in us."

Two paths are then open. The first is to accord a rational status to what is given as an existential and ineffable experience. Then the subject seeks to make it explicit by an equally *forensic* doctrine, one capable of sustaining the person and satisfying his natural desire to know. Thus there is born, *alongside* religious life, the practice of speculation, at first gnostic in the style of Boehme. Then, as this speculation settles and gradually is secularized, it gives rise to free philosophic speculation detached from dogma, but still marked by the dramatic seal of Lutheranism. Luther did not leave behind a speculative theology in the Catholic sense, but he opened up an important path to a conceptualized spirituality grounded in philosophy (Jaeger).

The other path transcends torment and seeks peace in the work of art. The mark of anxiety can be seen in the great paintings of Grünewald, Altdorfer, and Baldung Grien, which is then appeased in the work of Cranach and Durer—with Italy's help. Finally it reaches the path of green pastures in music. Bach, "the musical preacher of Lutheranism," who knows in his religious soul the distinctly Christian aspect of the personal relationship with God, colors it in his way with the dramatic character of Lutheranism. The contrapuntal form, of which he is the master, conveys the double experience that alternates between annihilation and salvation. He rejoices in the certainty of salvation and exalts it. In his cantatas the theme of joy is definitively victorious and the severe God is fulfilled in Christ as Savior. Bach composes masses.

Finally there is a third path, one in which the faithful will be engulfed en masse, that of feeling, of the heart, of piety. The pietist revolution overwhelms the Lutheran edifice of justification by faith by making piety the judge of faith. Faith flows from piety and not the reverse. Thus anxiety is swamped by sentimentalism, or by the communitarian fusion produced by the mass movement of Awakenings. Or, for certain religious, peacefully Christian souls, it is overcome by the delicious meditation of spiritual texts, either medieval or Protestant, and, as always, of the Bible.

Calvin's nature, according to what he confided, was timid, modest, reserved and little given to personal confidence. We know that his soul was already attacked by doubt in the horrible Collège of Montaigu where he was a pupil, and that in the following years he was practically obsessed by "a feeling of fragility, of weakness before a God who is primordially a just God and who weighs the good and evil of every creature" (Crouzet). *The Institutes of the Christian Religion,* which he published in Latin at the age of thirty and in French at thirty-three (1641), proves that he had definitively overcome his anxiety—that is, by the doctrine *soli Deo Gloria,* and by the associated ideas of predestination and sanctification.

The doctrine of predestination appears to Calvin himself as "strange and hard." He declares that even before the Fall, God, according to his eternal counsel, had decided to appoint some to salvation (grace is irresistible) and others to perdition, or reprobation, that is, hell. A disciple in Calvin's circle, Jerome Bolsec, publicly attacked him in 1551. He argued that the idea of predestination leads to making God responsible for human sins, the efficient cause of the evil acts of the damned. Calvin treated Bolsec like a charlatan and a pig and condemned him to banishment. After Calvin's death this doctrine was abandoned little by little, but very slowly. It was proclaimed by the first canon of the synod of Dort in 1618 and is still considered binding in certain churches. But we have seen that, far from causing anxiety among those who profess it, the mere fact of believing it and firmly professing it suffices to bring certainty that one is on the right side. To believe in it is to make the decision of an act of supreme confidence in God. Augustine believed that the elect, while contemplating the sinners amid eternal flames, rejoiced and worshiped God in his justice. Calvin does the same, "for these things are joined together and inseparable, that God has chosen us and that he now calls us to holiness."

Anguish is for other people, the camp of the condemned, and they have well deserved it, since all human beings merit reprobation, except those that it pleases God to choose all the same, gratuitously and by grace alone.

As for sanctification, it is a way of life under God's watchful eye. Man works and enjoys the legitimate goods he earns by this work as long as he refers all to God. He lives a disciplined life by following the law of the Decalogue, as the Holy Spirit enables him to discern it. Scripture is inspired, but to recognize this inspiration and to discern God's Word in scripture is a gift of the Holy Spirit. Whoever can recognize this double inspiration possesses the guarantee of his election. Work in itself brings peace. Did not Voltaire himself say, at the conclusion of *Candide*, that it serves to avoid vice, boredom and need? So much the better if it also brings a good conscience, the conviction that this work is sanctifying and keeps the faithful on the path of virtue. We must recognize that we owe this virtuous life to God. "Why must we do good works? Because," answers the Heidelberg Catechism, "Christ, having redeemed us by his blood, is also restoring us by his Spirit into his image, so that with our whole lives we may show that we are thankful to God for his benefits, so that he may be praised through us, so that we may be assured of our faith by its fruits, and so that by our godly living our neighbors may be won over to Christ." Thus the religion of *sola fide* becomes one of the most moralizing religions of all time.

Melanchthon wondered whether he was still dealing with Christianity, or with a Christianized stoicism (Bouyer). The work of sanctification must nevertheless be pursued throughout the whole of life. The virtues that may bring riches must still be practiced once these riches have been obtained. Thus one can find American billionaires living soberly, going to the office as long as their legs can still carry them and their eyes are good enough to read their accounts. But having "learned to be rich," they make good use of their goods. One of the sources of American philanthropy springs from Calvinist sanctification.

What becomes of one who does not practice the virtues, who is addicted to vices, who scandalizes his neighbors by his impiety and many sins? He has simply proved that his faith is manifestly false and that he is not saved. He has lost the right to participate in the sacrament of the Holy Supper. He is excommunicated from his Church. The grace of God is no longer with him. He is reprobate. The civil magistrate may punish him severely, and, because God does not love him, the elect have no need to love him either. "Christ taught his own to forgive and to suffer offenses. [...] Nevertheless this mildness and moderation of their courage will not mean that, while preserving complete love toward their enemies, they do not accept the comfort of the magistrate in conserving their well-being or that, for the public good, they do not demand the punishment of the perverse and noxious, who can only be corrected by punishment."

The work of sanctification fills a life, and this is why it has no need for the auxiliaries supplied, in Lutheran countries, by philosophy and art. One might say that the Calvinist is so busy with his task that he has no time for such things. And yet, there has been art. Calvin is intransigent on the point that the church must be naked and devoid of all religious imagery. But art as such is a human faculty that can be employed for the glory of God alone. It is also a work. It suffices to think of Dutch painting—without forgetting of course that it is not entirely Calvinist, that Rembrandt was not Calvinist, and that Vermeer was probably Catholic. There is no Calvinist music to speak of; the vigorous hymns sung in church have nothing in common with Bach's profound effusions or with Lutheran music. Calvinism nourished some great poetry, Aubigné in France and Milton in England. It did not give rise to a philosophical speculation supplementary to theology or inspired by it. Calvinist theology, following Calvin's own example, is oriented toward exegesis and a deeper understanding of the Word. It seeks as well the compatibility between the Word and reason. Calvinism thus opens itself to liberalism, by way of a pursuit of a reasonable religion, "within the limits of reason."

Can we say, then, that anxiety was overcome in the Calvinist world? No doubt, but at the cost of continual effort. It is ceaselessly pushed further off and deferred by the effort of sanctification. The result is a kind of overexertion that is spiritual as well as physical, since each believer takes on the whole duty of the priesthood including prayer, praise, instruction, and preaching. This is why many Protestants of the eighteenth century, feeling the exhaustion of this overexertion, so avidly welcomed the quietism of Fénelon and of Mme. Guyon. Fénelon helped them separate authentic Christianity from a kind of anarchic, adulterated, enthusiastic mysticism that was rampant in their ranks. Jurieu taught that true mysticism was nothing other than a scriptural and reasoned theology that renews the inner man (Jaeger). Fénelon, who was sometimes believed to have converted to Protestantism, wished in this way to purify papist mysticism, but without veering into *enthusiasm*. Neither Roman nor enthusiast, this mysticism lightens the load that bears down upon the Reformed believer.

The Roman Catholic Church disposed of a rich arsenal for addressing anxiety. It possessed an extraordinarily pompous, ornate liturgy, one that was rich with instruction. It offered sacraments. The Eucharist is taken to the highest degree of objectivity: Christ is truly present in the transubstantiated species, with which the believer *communes*, eventually under both species—the Church had just authorized it in Bohemia—which he can worship outside the services, carry in a procession, or take to the sick, for the presence is permanent. The Church claims the power of the keys, both by the sacrament and by penitence; it has the power to remit sins, however grave they may be. Finally it has constructed an immense edifice of systematic thought, which brings together practically, in a single discipline, the whole corpus of philosophy, from its beginnings through Plato, Aristotle, the Stoics and their posterity, and theological reflection since Irenaeus and Justin down to Saint Thomas, including that of the Church Fathers, Augustine, Anselm, and all the others.

And yet all this had not sufficed to calm the disquiet that had spread everywhere, nor to appease the anxiety of the most fervent souls, and there were none more fervent than those of Luther and Calvin. The Protestant territory spread ceaselessly, with the support of the people.

Where anxiety was concerned, the Catholic Church made use of whatever means it could find. It further developed the consoling, transfiguring, transporting possibilities of the most grandiose liturgy. It was able to adorn it with magnificent music, including Palestrina, Monteverdi, Charpentier, and Couperin. Eucharistic worship was extended. The art of confession—rigorist, lax, exact in indulgence as in severity—was carried to a point of perfection. It encouraged the explosion of Baroque art, which not only restored the image in the face of Protestant iconoclasm, but simultaneously exalted God, represented in every permissible way, as well as man, whom the Church considered by no means as corrupted to the root, but whom she exalted heroically by borrowing freely from ancient art forms. Without reducing the distance between them, this art presented at once God as the friend of man and the magnanimity of man in his response to God.

This was not enough to fulfill life and to put an end to anxiety. It must be said that the fundamental remedy to anxiety that characterizes the Catholic Church is the search for truth. It is an activity of the mind, which is made possible by the conviction that human reason, despite its limits, is capable of a rational discourse concerning God, and that God is knowable up to a point. Despite the radical unknowability of the divine being, there is a positive path to him, sustained by the supernatural means of grace and by the invocation of the Holy Spirit, but these in no way render vain the effort of the mind, which is capable of progress in knowledge. This quest is endless, but, like Calvinist sanctification, it fills a person's life and, perhaps better than Calvinism, it is able to bring a certain degree of peace. It is freer, and does not entirely take over one's life, but allows for intervals, though it must be taken up again whenever a cause of torment, or just a problem, arises. "A thousand difficulties do not make a doubt," Newman said. Difficulties are resolved by the intelligence of faith. Fideism and blind and unintelligent faith are not sustainable for long and are not authorized. The Catholic is in principle called to the pursuit of truth until the end of his earthly pilgrimage, at the end of which he hopes finally to discover it in its fullness.

This is a duty. But can we say that the Catholic Church was successful in accomplishing it as it sustained the attack of the Reformation?

It had to deal with some rough opponents. It suffices to pass a little time with Luther and with Calvin in order to be convinced that it was improbable that the Catholic world would find within itself personalities of this caliber. It did find some in the area of holiness. Saint Ignatius was not an intellectual. He had begun his spiritual adventure with the light equipment of an officer and a courtier of a little provincial court. Nevertheless, the Company that he founded proved to be the main breeding ground of the soldiers of Catholic intelligence. In the end the Protestant hemorrhaging was staunched.

The Catholic Reformation counter-attacked on all fronts. It clarified doctrine, and after the Council of Trent substantially recognized the *sola fide* and the *sola gratia*—but it was too late. The break was complete and Protestants no longer accepted the Church's interpretation, nor in particular its authority to interpret. It focused on metaphysics, a terrain that Protestantism had abandoned. With Suarez in Salamanca and Descartes in Paris it hoped to find an *aggiornamento* of its philosophical theology, heavily burdened by an Aristotelianism that no longer seemed relevant. That did not work. Suarez deformed Thomism without restoring either its plenitude or its persuasive power. Descartes owed much to the

Ockhamist tradition, and Malebranche still more, and their inter-locutors were authors such as Hobbes, Spinoza, and Leibniz, all strangers to Catholicism and detached from the doctrine approved by Rome. Higher thought, with the possible exception of Vico, no longer fit within the limits of Catholic orthodoxy, which it saw as confining.

The inspiration of the Catholic Reformation, especially in its Jesuit version, owed much to the Renaissance, to its humanism, its triumphant optimism and its joy. But at this juncture there arose within the Church the Jansenist disease. Its origin was in the North, in Louvain, close to the Calvinist frontier, and in Paris, the capital of a kingdom that had almost come over to this side and that held Rome at a distance.

From Calvinism Jansenism had received, despite its protesta-tions, whether sincere or not, if not the doctrine of double predes-tination, at least that of predestination itself. But it dissociated this doctrine from the certainty of salvation, which in Calvinism was joined to it.

The Catholic Church cannot accept the Protestant doctrine of the certainty of salvation. It sees human beings as on Jacob's ladder, climbing, coming down, tumbling, and climbing back up. It affirms that Christ died for all mankind, that the value of his redemption is universal and, moreover, that, where those lacking in virtue are concerned, it has received certain powers from God, all the means of salvation, if only they desire it. Predestination is inseparable from the benevolent plan that God has conceived for his creatures. Voltaire, whose father was Jansenist and brother affected by reli-gious convulsions, said, for once like a good Catholic, that he could not conceive of a God who would have created the world in order to send most human beings to hell. Thus, according to the good doctrine, on the one hand salvation is potentially universal and, on the other, personal salvation is uncertain, contingent up to the last hour. But if one joins together, as do the Jansenists, salvation re-served to certain men alone and the uncertainty of salvation, the adept is condemned to perpetual anguish. Whereas the Calvinist, confiding his salvation to God, looks straight ahead without turning around and attends to his vocation, the Jansenist is always looking into himself, asking whether he possesses the efficient or efficacious grace or whether he is among the number of the damned. He looks upon himself with suspicion, weighs his actions on the scale of vain self-love, and strives daily to attain virtue, all the while considering that it is of no worth, or even that it counts as a vice.

Lutheran anxiety contained a continuously renewed appeal to Christ as Savior and, as it became an inseparable component of the spiritual life, it happened that it became in itself a source of consolation. Calvinist anxiety is almost a sin, since it must normally be evacuated in the work of sanctification. There is nothing more sterile than Jansenist anxiety, for it does not even know whether the prayers that it addresses to the hidden God pleases him or whether it does not add one more seal to his perdition. The only benefit the Jansenist draws from it is an ever deeper and darker penetration into his necessarily guilty conscience, a kind of interminable psychoanalysis of his soul and of its bottomless abyss. And yet it produced a great literature.

But what a disaster for the Catholic Church! The greatest Catholic kingdom, the kingdom of France, was infected, and the contagion spread to Belgium, Italy, and Ireland, giving Christianity a severe, sad and moralizing aspect, worse than the worst of Protestantism, having lost the Catholic breadth, humanity and joy, but without the profound outlets of Lutheran mysticism, without music or mystique – Jansenism detests mysticism and hunts it down much more efficiently than in Protestant lands —, without as well the virile courage that causes the Calvinist pioneer, free and alone, to clear new lands. The Church sees a new front open up within itself. It is paralyzed by the interminable Jansenist contention. Its territory shrinks, and though baroque art survives in Bavaria and in Austria, and in the kingdom of Naples, these are not the areas where the pursuit of truth is the main concern. In the end Jansenism not only ruined Catholic piety, but that which went with it, the Ancien Régime in France and the Society of Jesus in Rome. It discouraged Christians and brought Paris over to the side of irreligion (Chaunu).

It is worth reflecting on this point: the mass apostasy from the Christian religion began in France, then in Italy, to the great scandal of the Protestant nations, England, Germany and the United States. The Jansenist crisis prepared the great Protestant triumph in Europe and in America that marked the nineteenth century. And this completed the fixing of anxiety upon the heart of the Catholic Church.

Luther's Political Theology

Luther's political theology was formed when his religious evolution had already ended. It took shape as events forced him to take a side, and these various and dramatic events were the product of the religious revolution that he had unleashed.

The medieval norm took it as a given that the Church was charged with progressively building the City of God along with the law that came from the temporal authority. Luther rejects this collaboration of the Gospel with the law. Law—not only that of Moses but earthly law in general—belongs to the world of sin. Nevertheless, Luther teaches us a Gospel morality that represents emancipation in relation to the law. Yet Saint Paul taught that authority is established by God. Luther, commenting on the Letter to the Romans in 1516, understands it in the most literal sense. "Wherever there is authority or it is exercised, it exists and is exercised because God instituted it." It is not for us to ask whether it is legitimate or not. All government is lawful. In this precocious text, Luther already provides one of the keys to his system: the distinction between the inner man, whose freedom is inherent, and external man, who is bound to servitude.

The theme is taken up more expansively in one of the three great early tracts of the Reformation, *On Christian Liberty* (1520). It is built on an antinomy. Religion's principle is faith, and its norm is freedom; morality's principle is love and its norm is servitude: "The Christian is a perfectly free lord of all things and is subject to none. The Christian is a perfectly dutiful servant of all and subject to all." According to the first part of the antinomy, faith is sufficient to the Christian. Having no need of any works, he is beyond doubt released from laws and precepts. And since he is released, he is free.

Another Lutheran concept, the universal priesthood, is grafted on at this point. Every believer receives the spiritual privileges that the Roman Church has wrongly arrogated to itself. These privileges are inherited directly from Christ. "As Christ possesses the honor and dignity of the first-born, he shares his advantages with all believers so that all may be kings and priests along with him." All Christians are thus "of a spiritual and ecclesiastical order, and there is no difference among them except what results from their responsibility." This responsibility is delegated by the community, stemming from a right possessed in common. Thus falls the "wall" of ecclesiastical authority. And what of princes? They cannot be denied the common privilege any more than another believer: "since he who exercises civil authority has received the same baptism and the same faith as we have, we cannot refuse him the title of priest or bishop, nor the privilege of considering his responsibility to be a Christian and spiritual office, one useful to the whole community" (*To the German Nobility*).

The first political consequence of the universal priesthood is thus a prodigious increase in the temporal authority, because it inherits the prestige of the priesthood which has been withdrawn from the ecclesiastical authority. The temporal power rules without counterweight or limitation and tends toward absolute sovereignty. Society constitutes a body of which Jesus is the head. But "Jesus does not have two bodies, one spiritual and the other secular." Nor is there more than a single head and a single body. This body is entirely subject here below to the civil authority: "This is why it is necessary that the civil authority, established by God to punish the wicked and protect the good, exercise its duty freely, without regard for appearances, throughout the whole body of Christendom, even if it should strike as needed against popes, priests, nuns, or anyone." Half-spiritual (having Christ as its head), half-temporal because it is a body, "Christendom" survives the collapse of the Church, but subject to an all-powerful civil government, left alone to exercise its function (Mesnard). Because the priesthood in the equality of believers allowed the prince to take on the role of the spokesman of the community, the temporal inequality of the faithful allows him to be the authorized expression of the universal priesthood and also to exercise a spiritual authority.

The pace of events quickens. Of course Luther always supported authority and order; still he stirred up the nobles to reject Rome's emissaries, to seize the Church's property, and the monks and nuns to renounce their vows and marry. Thus was unleashed the peasant war that ruined a third of Germany and that ended with an immense massacre of the insurgents. So he writes the *Treatise on Secular Authority: Up to What Point Must One Obey?*

The two canonical texts of Paul (Romans 13:1) and Peter (2:13) remain the pillars of the divine origin of civil authority. The Old Testament presents Cain as guilty and conscious of having violated justice, and Moses as founding the *lex talionis* that subjects the Jews to the sword of justice. But what is to be done with the text of Matthew that advises turning the other cheek, and that of Paul that advises not defending oneself but leaving things to God's wrath? Luther answers that the first commandments are the law of the world and the others (which for him are commandments and not counsel) the law of Christ. True Christians can practice evangelical detachment, because they are not of the world and have no need either of a sword or of any legal order. They bear injustice joyously. But as for the others, the unjust, "they need the law to teach them, constrain them and cause them to do good."

For Luther, no human being is good by nature. None are righteous; there are only those who are justified. The law of the world includes practically all men, even if a little flock of the elect is in theory capable of governing itself by Christ's law. Against the Anabaptists who claimed to do away with the sword and to obey only the inspiration of the Holy Spirit, Luther means to leave the two governments side by side, that of the Spirit and that of earthly princes. The first recruits volunteers; the second, one is forced to enter.

Who bears the sword? Those who have the calling, as one has the calling to be a shoemaker or a farmer. It is an office that must be honored. And it must be obeyed with generosity, because the State is the context in which charity is normally exercised. Let the Christian collaborate in the State's existence, as in every work of love; let him pay taxes and lend aid to authorities. The sword protects the good, of course, but mainly it strikes the wicked. "You may ask if executioners, valets and jurists [...] can be Christians and attain salvation in this state. Answer: if power and the sword are in the service of God [...] then all that is necessary to power in order to apply the sword is also in the service of God."

Soldiers are like surgeons who amputate some members in order to save the whole body. This is why "God instituted war and the slitting of throats," which, despite appearances are "a work of love."

Secular authority is just and providential. Christian freedom forbids the prince to impose his beliefs on his subjects; he would thus lead them to eternal death. God will punish this pretension, to which the subject must oppose a passive and respectful resistance. That said, one must not resist violence to oneself but suffer persecution for the sake of faith. This is Luther's position in 1520. But over the following years, he understood the necessity of forming a new church. But a church is not a purely spiritual community, governed by the word of God alone. It comes to be modeled more and more closely on the political community. Thus we find him demanding the intervention of the secular power and, once this step is taken, he sees no way to limit its effects. Next he asks the prince, if he cannot oppose heresy, at least to prevent the ongoing sacrilege represented in the Mass, this scandalous return to the law. If the Mass were tolerated, God's wrath would fall upon the land. The prince as a diligent Christian brother must uphold the faith. Luther also wants the municipal councils in the communes to play a role in the nomination of pastors. In 1525, he asks the Elector to organize a "visitation" of parishes and to name certain persons to inspect the Church. This again is a duty of charity rather than a secular function proper. Soon Luther will ask him to "put down the savage beasts" (Anabaptists) who refuse to accept the new order of things, in particular the unity of worship. In fact, the

Elector, as the lord of the land, has become responsible for both the spiritual and the temporal good of his subjects. Having accepted the intervention of the sword in spiritual affairs, as well as the link between political authority and the form of worship in the territory under this authority, Luther had in fact adopted Melanchthon's formula, which will later be that of the whole Lutheran Church: "It is the subject's duty, where religion is concerned, to rely on the wisdom and competence of the prince."

It is understood that the prince is Christian. But Luther's pessimism is such that he does not want this prince to govern according to law and respect for customs. As is well known, Luther has no use for jurists, or for privileges or constitutions. The prince must govern like Solomon, who set aside the counsels and even the law of Moses: "He must appeal to God alone, speak in his ear, ask him to administer his subjects wisely, above and beyond books and teachers, with an upright intelligence."

Before and after the peasant war, Luther clarifies his thought. In anger, he hardens again and talks in a way so close to that of Ivan the Terrible, at the end of the century in his correspondence with Kourbski, that one might ask if there is not some parallelism, or, by unexamined channels, some influence. "The civil power, a minister of divine wrath over the wicked and a true precursor of hell and of eternal death, must not be merciful, but unbending, severe, and wrathful in its function and its work, for his badge is not a rosary or a flower of love, but a naked sword."

Subjects possess no right of rebellion. Pagans glorified tyrannicide, but Christians know that temporal government is a divine order, or in any case respectable. Rebellion not only destroys all authority, but it is an offense against God. All rebellion is a case of lèse-majesté against God, an attack on his sovereignty. For Luther there is no political or social contract: authority comes by simple divine delegation. There is no reciprocity between the prince and the people. Political hierarchy is established with the emperor at its summit, then the princes, then the nobles, and finally the vulgar. Each obeys and commands within the hierarchical chain, and the man of the people is left with only the resource of absolute command in his home.

Luther's original intention was to destroy papal authority and that of the ecclesiastical hierarchy. His first step is therefore to rehabilitate the civil authority. The two sources from which he drew his theory, Justinian and the Bible, he finds in agreement in denying the State as a community of citizens and affirming it as authority and power. This State may be viewed as a *Volksstaat*, as long as the people are understood as a passive prime matter, organized and commanded by the political hierarchy, no citizen being able to escape its authority or affirm any kind of individualism. If the prince acts as a tyrant, this is because he is conducting himself as an executioner; the people are guilty and need the punishment they have merited.

The humanist prince believed in natural virtues and free will. He aimed at the temporal common good and guided public life toward its natural good. The Lutheran prince lives in fear of being a sinner and governs a world of sin. The State loses its proper function which, according to classical philosophy, is the pursuit of natural laws and of the common good. This function is subordinated to that of realizing ideal ends, those proposed by the *Kulturstaat*. The enlightened despot of the Enlightenment was optimistic concerning both himself and his political action. But Luther does not believe in the existence of such an enlightened despot. "Princes are usually the most mad of men and the most arrant bandits in the world. That's why, with them, we must always foresee the worst and expect little good, especially concerning divine things that require care for souls." Pierre Mesnard is right to conclude that it is not possible to build a positive and felicitous politics on a metaphysics such as Luther's that holds that "God cast us into the world under the power of the devil." "We cannot wish to reform a world in which Evil is sovereign."

Calvin's Political Theology

Compared to Luther, who pushes Augustinian pessimism to the point of despair, Calvin looks like an optimist. He separates himself from his greater predecessor on three main points. He definitively posits the principle of freedom of conscience. He maintains the independence of the Church in relation to the state. And he holds that the State can be governed by Christian principles.

The 1541 edition, in French, of *The Institutes of the Christian Religion* fixed the position of Calvinists on political matters. It opens with a preface and dedication to King Francis I: "To the Most High, Most Powerful, Most Illustrious Prince, Francis, the Most Christian King of France, His Prince and Sovereign Lord, peace and salvation in God from John Calvin." The tone is set: on the one hand, deference and just submission to a legitimate prince; on the other, dignity and independence as citizen and Christian. The end of this preface reads like this: "May the Lord King of Kings establish your throne in justice and your office in equity, most mighty and illustrious King." Here the citizen's dignity rises to the remonstrance of and salutary warning of the prophet.

This preface was published just after the dreadful burnings at the stake that followed the provocation of the *"placards."* These were posters ridiculing the Mass which had been posted at the king's very chambers by sectarian Protestants, and which had put an end to the humanist hope for Catholic reform in France. Calvin means to clear the Protestants of blame for sedition. He affirms, moreover, that their doctrine is not new, since it is none other than the pure Gospel. Was not Christ seditious in the eyes of the Jews? Calvin affirms his loyalty and condemns the revolutionaries, while noting the civic superiority of the Reformed; these will remain the positions of Calvinist politics everywhere.

Calvin condemns the Anabaptists, not only because their rejection of sexual norms leads to scandal, but because they are theologically mistaken. They claim to follow the free inspiration of the Holy Spirit. This is "frenzy." The Holy Spirit "is given to us as a sanctification to lead us to conduct ourselves in obedience to God's justice, having purged us of foulness and filth." The human spirit, which is entirely "blocked off from spiritual things," is not corrupted to the point of being incapable of recognizing truths in earthly things. "There is no one who does not acknowledge that all assemblies of human beings must be governed by some law and

that there is some principle of such law in his understanding."
There is in all human beings some "seed of political order," and no
one is "destitute of reason where the government of the present life
is concerned."

As a Christian, however, he knows that all law must be related
analogically to divine law. This is supernatural and is inscribed in
two ways, in our conscience and in the holy books. The Calvinist
citizen does not lose sight of the cause of God, obedience to God
above all, even where the humblest temporal reality is concerned.
This law, which Christ did not abrogate but restored and made it
possible to understand in its entirety, is the Decalogue. The fifth
commandment, which enjoins us to honor our father and mother,
may be understood in an extended sense: "The end is: that God
wills that the order that he has instituted be maintained, that we
must observe the degrees of preeminence as he has established
them." This commandment puts us in the right way politically. The
reverence that is due to our father and to our superior leads us to
reverence for God, who is the sovereign Father. Authority deserves
respect—but only so long as it organizes society in such a way as
to lead us to rise toward the Father and the practice of his commandments. All power comes from God. But power exists only in
order to lead men to God. Here Calvin diverges from the natural
ends of politics.

Calvin seems on this point not so far from Erasmus or from
Catholic doctrine, except on one particular: the Church. In effect,
according to the tradition, the precepts of faith and of reason, both
of which have their origin in the divine Word, are manifest on the
earth by means of the temporal power enlightened by the commandments of the Church. The people's execution of precepts
comes about through the organ of a temporal Christianity bound
up with a visible, hierarchical, and centralized Church. But this is
not how Calvin conceives the Church.

For Calvin, the Church consists in "all those who are chosen
by the providence of God." It is thus one, holy and eternal. But no
visible Church fits this definition. The true Church is known by
God alone. Calvin accepts another definition that is still canonical:

"Wherever we see the Word of God being purely preached and heard and the sacraments administered as Christ instituted them, there, it must in no way be doubted, is the Church." But still, the Churches so defined are of very different value and purity. They have the right to disagree on doctrine up to a point, and concerning morals "we must not be too difficult." The Cathars and the Donatists are Christians. Even the Roman abominations leave baptism and the divine covenant intact. Thus all degrees exist between Rome and the pure reformed Church. It follows that the Church cannot be a body that claims to incarnate the spiritual unity of Christians. It is a society of spirits, or rather a multitude of societies of spirits.

Calvin fears the excesses of the Anabaptist movement and the lawless tendencies arising from it. God's law, which is the same and continuous from the days of the ancient patriarchs to Jesus Christ, is in the service of sanctification. Nevertheless, justification itself is not obtained by obedience to the law, but by free grace. So it is that the conscience "rises and lifts itself above the law and forgets all of the justice of the law" in order to enter directly into divine mercy. Obedience to the law must not be an outward conformity, but a free confidence toward God himself.

The conscience of one who has become a child of God and is liberated by the blood of Christ is "free and exempt from the power of men." In this way Calvin solemnly proclaims freedom of conscience.

Conscience is free in the face of the Catholic ecclesiastical power that usurps its role in desiring to govern it. The Church's authority must be limited to the preaching of the Word. Catholics do not have the right to dictate binding laws or to make themselves judges of faith. Ecclesiastical discipline, which Calvin nevertheless judges necessary, does not obligate the conscience and is limited to causing a "rule of honesty" to be respected.

But if conscience is an inviolable fortress, it can very well accommodate a tyrannical government in the temporal domain. Like all the political thinkers of his generation, whether Catholic or Lutheran, Calvin rejects the right of rebellion. Not until Calvinists are seriously persecuted will they accept the right of resistance to the tyrant, and even the right to kill him. Persecution will also bring Catholics, equally loyalist in principle, over to the side of tyrannicide. Calvin is a loyalist even toward bad governments, because they come from God. Spiritual freedom can very well coexist with civil servitude. But he is not Lutheran in the sense of regarding social and political action as essentially foreign to Christians. Nor does he agree with the Anabaptists, who see politics as inherently sinful. Civil society has modest aims, such as rendering men obliging and respectful. It is an indispensable environment for human beings, like air, water and sun. It makes material prosperity possible. But in the eyes of the Eternal, its goals are higher: it must provide for the protection of human justice, the well-being of the true religion, and prevent blasphemy and idolatry. Thus, from God's point of view, it is necessary to political concord and, further, it is competent to enforce the correct religious establishment and to punish evil-doers.

There are three "parts" of civil society: "The first is the Magistrate, who is the guardian and preserver of laws. The second is the Law, according to which the Magistrate rules. The third is the People, who must be governed by the laws and obey the Magistrate."

Calvin relies on the Bible to justify the divine origin of authority—the whole Bible, the Old Testament as much as the New, and always without any historical perspective, except that the New Testament allows us better to understand the Old. The Bible is a timeless whole. Magistrates, according to the examples he draws from the kings and prophets of Israel, had received the mandate of "rewarding the good and punishing the wicked." This second duty is agreeable to God: "Their true justice is to persecute the wicked with an unrestrained sword." If they wish in this area to keep their "hands clean," then they are guilty of great injustice. Calvin does not bother with the form of government: monarchy, government by "the respectable," popular power—all have their advantages and disadvantages.

The law is a "silent magistrate" and the magistrate is a "living law." Calvin does not hold to the literal requirements of the "Hebrew laws," but simply that the law be just and conformed to God's reasonable will. Thus he introduces, despite his attachment to the principle of loyalism, the idea of equity that will later be available, when persecution comes, as a basis for the conscientious rejection of unacceptable laws.

As for the people, their duty is to acquiesce willingly and joyfully to authority. They must obey not out of fear but from reverence and love. Calvin rejects the Anabaptist thesis of conscientious objection and upholds the Pauline thesis of conscientious adherence. The prince is *a priori* beneficent. If he is tyrannical or unjust, we must still obey him, by an act of faith in divine providence. Under the administration of the good prince as well as under the reign of the tyrant, we are to feel the hand of God and revere it. Providence alone has the right to dash the wicked tyrant's scepter, as we see in the Bible when a bad king drives out another bad king, or when a prophet overturns for an instant the duty of obedience, by a sort of political miracle and by an express delegation from God. But this case is exceptional and does not constitute a rule: "Every private person who violates a tyrant is explicitly condemned by the voice of God."

This, then, is Calvin's position before his approach to a position of power. He juxtaposes the inalienable freedom of conscience with an absolute political loyalism that is even pushed to the point of heroism, because it is necessary to the natural order.

In Germany, a Christian people had shaken off the yoke of the Church only to fall under that of more selfish and burdensome princes. Among Zwingli's followers in Geneva, Bern, and Zurich, above parish-level democracy or the assembly of the faithful, it is the municipal councils who elect pastors and provide for the common discipline. Everywhere councils are taking spiritual direction in hand.

Calvin's decisive originality lies in not having accepted this form of governance. As soon as he arrives in Geneva, in 1537, he demands a systematic organization of the Church and that the "Confession of God" become a condition of access to bourgeois status.

In effect he requires civil society to recognize his doctrine of faith as a monopoly. The following year, the council refuses and decides to open the Sacrament of the Holy Supper to all who request it, which is equivalent to refusing this monopoly. Calvin must go into exile.

At this point Calvin understands clearly the need to remove the Church from secular domination and for this purpose to provide a new organization, the core of which will be a body of solidly educated pastors. When he returns, in 1541, he requires the acceptance of *The Ordinances of Geneva*. These affirm the principle of religious unity: everyone is required to "swear by the faith," that is, the faith contained in *The Institutes of the Christian Religion*. The community of the faithful is disempowered in favor of the body of pastors. A new minister is recruited by fellow ministers and proposed to the people for their acceptance; he becomes minister only by the laying on of hands, which can only be administered by pastoral authority. Finally, ecclesiastical discipline as a whole is confided to a new body, the consistory. This is a mixed body where both the pastors and the members of the council of the republic of Geneva are represented. There follows a struggle that will last ten years between the council and the hierarchy of pastors. When the "Elders" predominate over the "Doctors" of the Church, it is the civil authority that prevails; when it is the "Doctors," it is the supremacy of the spiritual domain and the freedom of the Church. Calvin manages to succeed by gradually enclosing the civil power under his repressive jurisdiction. He makes attendance at sermons and schools mandatory, which spreads the Calvinist teaching to the whole country. He requires laws to be passed against gambling, dancing, luxury, and immorality. Beginning in 1561, Elders are no longer selected only from the councils, but from the whole population, which is already controlled by the pastors, a development that might also be interpreted as a kind of decline of traditional elites and a step toward democratization. Calvin, who holds no office or employment, is henceforth the complete master of the city, by the mere authority of his person. At the center of the system there thus stands Calvin's exceptional charisma. The pastors rally solidly around him. Next there is the consistory, made up of ministers and elders, a deliberative assembly and a tribunal, which prepares regulations, oversees worship, calls for fasts, judges conflicts, and pronounces penalties. Finally there are the people, raised in Calvinist temples and schools, who oversee the aristocracy of the councils and ratify no election, whether of a pastor or an elder, that is contrary to the Word.

One might speak of a kind of democratic centralism, if the expression had not been prostituted by modern totalitarian regimes. In Geneva Calvin had founded a counterfeit democratic republic, one dominated in fact by the aristocracy of councils. He was satisfied to control it by the more open assembly of citizens. He was not able to attain the theocracy he would have liked, which would have been similar to the Jesuit government ("reductions") in Paraguay, with the whole population at work, disciplined, divided up, recreated according to regulation. The councils did not submit. On the other hand – and this is the great contribution of Calvinism—there arose a sense of civic equality in obedience to the law. The Lutheran civil magistrate was naturally a preeminent member of the Church. The Genevan civil magistrate left his badges at the door of the consistory. Christian equality here takes practical effect because the dignity of each citizen is recognized. Thus a door is opened to freedom under law, to modern democracy. It will flourish in America.

The Calvinist Churches

In France, the Calvinist ecclesiastical organization was conceived all at once by Calvin and adopted by the clandestine synod of 1559. It is here that one can best see in their purity the main ideas that govern this organization. There are six of them (Crouzet).

The first is equality. Churches are equal and so are their ministers. "No Church may assume primacy and domination over another." The same goes for ministers: they will take turns presiding over the consistory.

The second is the arbitration that is provided for the provincial synods. Each Church sends a minister and an elder (or a deacon) chosen by the local consistory. A national synod can pronounce on doctrine, disciplinary infractions, and censures.

The third is election, but this is determined by the criterion of respectability. The consistory elects the pastor; the people give their consent. The one elected signs a confession of common faith and receives the laying on of hands of functioning ministers. He is then minister for life, but he can be deposed and even excommunicated by the provincial consistory.

The fourth is the delegation of authority. This is retained by the elders and deacons who constitute the consistory, under the presidency of the ministers of the Word. To the elders falls the oversight of the Church. The deacons are responsible for charity and must go from house to house catechizing believers. They cannot preach or administer the sacraments, but can "assist."

The fifth concerns excommunication. This punishes heresy, insult to God's honor, rebellion against the consistory, and treason against the Church. It is also pronounced against criminals and those who cause scandal. It may be public or confidential. The Church of the Saints is the Church of honest, decent people. It is not like the old Church, the Church of the good and the wicked: "Let not persons of bad conduct be counted among the number of Christians, to God's great displeasure, as if the Church were a receptacle for the wicked and evil-living. For, since the Church is the body of Christ, it must not be corrupted by polluted members, lest a part of the shame come upon the Head. In order that there be nothing in the Church that might bring any dishonor upon God's name, all those who might by their turpitude defame and dishonor Christianity must be driven away."

The sixth has to do with the supervision of social life: the repression of blasphemy and of lewdness, but also the recording of baptisms, the inscription of the names of parents and god-parents, and the regulation of marriage. Marriage must be approved by the consistory, which inspects the contract concluded before the notary. The consent of parents is required, though exceptions are admitted. The whole of life is thus enveloped in the Church.

One might say that, with Calvinism, Protestantism, at first a confused movement, a kind of eruption of prime matter, found its form. The anxiety concerning salvation seems to be quieted. "With the later Calvin after 1545, the period of the essentially soteriological Reformation, centered on the preoccupation with Salvation, has more or less come to an end. The preoccupation with the Church returns to the surface" (Chaunu). Now the faithful are looking for a structure in which they can live and find shelter. Calvin proposes a Church to them, which he considers an authentic return to the Church of the time of apostles, elders, bishops, and the people. It is offered as an alternative Church, the true Church of the elect, in the face of the false Church, the Catholic Church, more than ever sunk into its abominations after the Council of Trent.

Luther's abandonment of communities to their natural princes made Lutheranism a German affair. This is to say that all sorts of passions inherited from history were mixed into the new faith: the frustrations of the empire, Ghibelline resentment of Rome and the Italians, and the utopianism of the Reich. Thus Lutheranism's expansion was limited to the sphere of these passions. Scandinavia came over to the Reformation somewhat clandestinely, as the princes in a way hid it from the people by preserving for some time the façade of Catholic worship.

Calvinist ecclesiology is, on the contrary, pure and stripped of all inherited impediments. It is in the strict sense "revolutionary." The ecclesial community is a *city on a hill,* as the American Puritans will put it. The doctrine makes no exceptions for local nationalisms. It is internationalist. It applies everywhere, in aristocratic circles (as in Hungary), among craftsmen and city-dwellers (as in Switzerland and England), and in mixed circles, as in France. It can and does spread everywhere. The model of Calvin's *Institutes* is taken up faithfully in summary form by various national Confessions. One of the first is the *Confessio Hungarica* of 1557. In Hungary, as in Poland, Calvinists swept away the too-German Lutheranism. The *Confessio Gallica* dates from 1557, "formatted" on the Calvinist model along with the *Confession de la Rochelle,* from 1571. Then comes the *Confessio Belgica*, which governs the Reformed of Holland. All receive the approbation of the all-powerful consistory in Geneva, the head of the Calvinist international (Le Roy Ladurie).

So solid is the organization Calvin developed, combining so harmoniously the ministry of the Word, the authority of the Elders, and the final arbitration of the People, that it will be able to perpetuate itself after the Calvinist faith has cooled, and even when its doctrine will be diluted or abandoned. It will stand all by itself because of its structural efficacy, like a governmental technique that has become autonomous in relation to the original convictions that brought about its birth—and also because it is adapted to the evolution of the modern society that it has accompanied and in part guided.

Staying Protestant

For about a century there was a give and take between Catholics and Protestants. Poland, Hungary, and Bohemia oscillated and in the end fell back, at least for the most part, on the Catholic side. The expansion of Protestantism in France met its stopping point at the Saint Bartholomew's Day massacre, and afterwards fell back until it was reduced to a little minority, stable but indomitable. England, Scotland, and the Scandinavian countries preserved only small and suspect cells of Catholics. The Thirty Years War fixed definitive borders in Europe. They would stay in place until the middle of the twentieth century.

It is an historical fact that schisms, heresies, religious creations or whatever they may be called result in extraordinarily solid crystallizations. A dictionary of Christian "heresies" (which of course is not how their adepts would refer to them) would run easily to two or three hundred entries. It is rare if there is not some little flock somewhere in the world that obstinately carries its flag. It is the same in Islam and Judaism. There are still some Samaritan villages in the Holy Land. It is also notable that heresies correspond to fault lines that affect specifically a given religious terrain, and that similar ones may re-emerge under different names, or else alter themselves subtly without exhibiting an explicit orthodoxy. For example, in Christianity, Arianism comes back in diverse configurations throughout history. From one age to another Modalism, Monophysitism, Nestorianism, Monothelitism, Pelagianism, work their ways beneath the surface of orthodoxy; they disappear, reappear, sometimes dormant and sometimes bringing about a crisis.

The Christian religion is particularly unstable. It issues from a revolutionary revelation, one far beyond what the religious and intellectual culture of its audience was capable of receiving. It urgently needed in a very short space of time to equip itself with an organized Church, a liturgy, a canon, and a doctrine. The task of this last was to provide the most correct interpretation of the faith. The task proved to be not impossible but endless. Christian doctrine chases a complete expression of the faith asymptotically without ever being able to claim a definitive match. Neither the Church Fathers, nor Saint Augustine, nor Saint Thomas attained perfect syntheses, and the Church has not committed wholly to any of them.

In comparison with Judaism Christianity lacks two solid anchoring points—the Torah fixed down to the very letter, considered to have "come down from Heaven" and sacralized by its commentators, and the support of a particular people defined by this same Torah. To be sure the Christian Scriptures represent its supreme authority. But it is clearly affirmed that they do not come directly from God in the manner of the Koran or even of the Torah. Their authors are inspired men. This is to say that the critical work of intelligence does not stop at the threshold of the inviolable Torah, but has the right to enter into Scripture itself. There has been and there is still in Protestantism a certain tendency to give the Scriptures the status of an immediate word of God. This has also been the case in Catholicism. But the right of investigation remains and even becomes a duty, such that in modern times we have seen a gradual destruction of the authority of the Scriptures at the hands of the very persons who intended only to scrutinize the text more closely and attain a more authentic meaning. Moreover there are no defined contours that set off the Christian people. It is always divided into nations, and it crumbles into irreducibly individual styles not exhaustively defined by Christian adherence, since the order of Christianity cannot be identified with a city of man.

The first prop devised by Christian orthodoxy to mitigate these two weaknesses was recourse to political power. It was not in vain that Constantine had bestowed upon him by the Church the title "equal to the apostles," having failed to get the one he wanted, "equal to Christ." The emperor, who had been responsible only for the material wellbeing of his subjects, now took on their spiritual salvation. The *Compelle Intrare*, in Augustine's interpretation, now assumed the very concrete meaning of an obligation to convert. The emperor designated patriarchs, convened councils, sometimes in his own palace, and guided them toward conclusions that seemed best to him. The compromise concluded with the Church meant that the Church conferred upon the emperor and on the kings who would succeed him the sacred legitimacy that surrounded David and the kings of Israel, and that in return the imperial and royal power committed itself to protecting the Church, to imposing orthodoxy as well as the appropriate moral norms. Emperors and kings renewed this commitment by an oath at their coronations.

This compromise lasted as long as the Eastern Empire. In the West the Empire crumbled and, unlike the Chinese Empire, was never able to reconstitute itself. This is why the question of orthodoxy took on new importance, because, since the unity of the Church could not be preserved from outside by the unity of the Empire, it had to be preserved by meticulous adhesion to the common doctrine. The Church had succeeded, after long struggles, if not to free itself completely, at least to avoid being absorbed by secular powers. It had its own power network, its sovereign territory, its intellectual centers, its shared culture, and its recognized orthodoxy. But this internal unity could not survive in the long run given the gradual fragmentation of pre-national Europe. The crumbling that the Thomistic synthesis was subject to is significant here, because the disputes in the universities and the springing up of new schools of thought and of piety that followed the fall of Thomism began gradually to reflect the self-assertion of emerging nations and to draw from their conflict. Once the unity of doctrine was lost, the Church preserved only a part of the domain that assured its independence and power. And even this domain was weakened by the increasing strength of secular powers.

The old conflict between these powers and the Church turned decisively to the benefit of the former beginning in the fourteenth century, because orthodoxy, a more and more ideal form of Christian unity, was no longer capable of imposing itself over the whole of this divided Europe. The unity of orthodoxy was a compensation for the growing multiplicity of the European continent. When this was broken, at the beginning of the sixteenth century, princes asserted their power in the spiritual realm as well as the temporal.

Luther had practically given the Church back to the princes; or rather he had considered that political communities could be considered spiritual communities. The prince is a "natural bishop." In England, the king proclaims his religious "supremacy." Scandinavia goes over to Protestantism by pure royal authority. Even in Catholic countries Rome's power is diminishing. In France the concordat signed by Leo X practically grants to Francis I the right to nominate bishops and thus the control of the Church—or at least so he believed, for it immediately united against royal power. Spain and Portugal obtained the "patronat" over new Churches in their empires. There kings did whatever they wanted.

In the Calvinist world, the decision to join the Reformation was taken by local powers, responding, up to a point, to the wishes of the people, or with their consent. In a fine monograph on the village Vébron in the Cévennes, Robert Poujol shows us how the new faith took root. Theodore Beza reports that, in this rude and harsh land, one "that might seem the least capable of receiving the Gospel by the rudeness of spirit of its inhabitants," these people nonetheless received "the truth of the Gospel with marvelous ardor, and they were joined not only by all of the commoners, but also by the gentlemen and the great lords." How was this so? Conversion took place by collective deliberation in the village's public place. Society was organized hierarchically, and the passage to the Reformation did not undo this order. By choosing the Reformation the upper class and the educated brought the whole population with them. The whole social body "espoused" the new religion. From that day on it supported the pastor and the temple. The parish priest left, or cast off his cassock. Tithes were confiscated for the Reformed Church (Poujol). This was not yet a matter of conscious and deliberate embrace of the Protestant faith, but only an agreement in principle. Nevertheless, it would eventually shape souls. And later nothing, neither Catholic missions nor less still the persecutions that followed the Revocation, could remove it. A conversion at first formal became real.

Thus throughout Europe temporal authorities dominate or become spiritual authorities. In the countries that remain Catholic the pope retains a certain authority, but he is marginalized by kings. In Protestant lands, the devolution is complete. In Calvinist lands there is a new kind of assumption of power. The hard core of pastors and doctors of the Church dominate the alternative organization that Calvinism offers, and this then strives to impose its norms on the civil powers. In this new situation, religious affiliation becomes a matter of political loyalty. Orthodoxy, whatever it may be, becomes a test of submission to legitimate power, for no one disputes the source of all power in God. Tocqueville notes that under Henry VIII anyone who strayed from the path, whether as Catholic or Lutheran, ran a strong risk of having to choose between being burned as a heretic or eviscerated as a traitor. And in Geneva itself, as shown by the Servetus affair, the Council of the Republic followed the advice of the consistory and sometimes even went beyond it. There were some condemnations to death for simple adultery.

Protestants are therefore Protestants, for the most part, because a political power said so. This power is in charge of ecclesiastical organization and thus of the religious education of its subjects. Why does one remain Protestant, from this perspective? Because it is the religion of one's country, where one was born, that of one's superiors, of one's nanny and parents. To be Protestant is a given, a *habitus*, from which there is no reason to remove oneself in the absence of serious and personal reflection on one's reasons for being such, which is only undertaken by a small minority. These are the same reasons that make a person a Catholic on the other side of the border.

A Protestant by habit, heredity, or custom has no need for an active passion. Still, in view of the Reformation's capacity to establish itself over time, it is impossible to deny the role of a lively passion, one called patriotism or nationalism, or in any case a primitive or already well-developed form of this modern passion. Luther is a fervent German. He embraces all the Ghibelline passions. Germany as a whole retained bitter memories of the innumerable maneuvers by which papal Italy had exploited, manipulated, divided and robbed it. The Lutheran Reformation appropriated this mass of resentments. Likewise, in England, papal politics, blindly allied with Spain, put what remained of a Catholic people among the bourgeoisie and the nobility in an untenable position, at least in the absence of exceptional courage. Calvinist internationalism is in principle detached from national allegiance. But in Geneva's confrontation with the Duke of Savoy, as in Holland's with the Duke of Alba and Scotland's with the English, religion made common cause with the national community and in great measure gave it its form. It must also be pointed out immediately that the same phenomenon appeared in symmetrical circumstances to make Catholicism the national religion of the Irish and the Poles.

The secular power of emperors, kings and princes was a force external to the Churches, in principle neutral in relation to the faith, even if it tried to use the faith for its political interests. National passions represent an intrusive force from below, one that is spontaneous, pregnant and much more difficult to separate intellectually from religious faith. This is the case in Orthodox countries, where the contours of the Churches blend officially with those of the Church and where, despite cautions against "phyletism," it is not clear whether the liturgical incense does not rise up toward the national entity as well as toward the God of Israel. It has been said that in Russia everything national became religious and everything religious became national. We consider that in England, where the political-religious nexus is tight, the faith can vanish without any diminution of attachment to the Church of England, or especially of innate distrust toward papal power over the faithful. The idea that Catholics "obey the Pope" is still today deeply rooted in Ulster, indeed in the whole kingdom. This is why Locke expressly excluded Catholics from the tolerance he wished to apply to all the Protestant confessions. This same theme of Catholic obedience to a foreign power served as an argument in Bismarck's *Kulturkampf* and in French Republican anti-clericalism. It was strong in the United States up to the twentieth century.

However one became Protestant, whether by heredity, custom, or personal choice, the person developed a particular sensibility that struck deep roots. In a country like France, where Protestants are an often endogamous minority, they tend to retain a style or bearing, almost a recognizable physical or behavioral type. As for Catholics, it is important to understand what surprises and shocks them.

Lutherans find Catholic piety superficial, its relation to Christ external, its process of salvation magic and its mass sacrilegious. The Calvinist cannot stand the jumble of idolatrous images that are heaped up in its churches. It is shocked by the pious anthropomorphism in speaking of God, or by the practice of using the same expressions indifferently in speaking of God and of the saints. The worship of Mary seems to the Calvinist to detract from the worship rendered to God alone. The confidence invested in ascetic practices, mystical experiences, rituals, fixed prayers and sacraments appear to be a way for man to appropriate a power that rightly belongs only to the sovereign action of the Word of God alone. "Idolatry and magic: these two reproaches levelled continuously by all Protestants against Catholics, which seem absurd to Catholics, hold such importance for Protestants because they appear as the inevitable counterpart to a sense of the greatness and holiness of God, the profound authenticity of which Catholics very rarely manage to grasp, deceived as they are by appearances to which they are not accustomed" (Bouyer). A Catholic who enters a Protestant Church finds it uninhabited. The sacred is nowhere to be found. The "reserved sacrament" is not practiced even in the most Catholic-friendly high Anglican Church, and one looks in vain in a sanctuary for the luminous point that signals to the faithful the invisible real presence behind the door of a tabernacle. This is intentional in the Reformation, which wishes to make it known that in effect there is nothing sacred in the temple. Beginning in the sixteenth century the temple was closed during services. It is simple and without ornament. The communion table is an ordinary dining room table. But the sacred inhabits the Protestant soul in the most authentically biblical and Christian form. The sense of God, of his greatness and "holiness" (in the sense of a transcendence, an elevation, an absolute "setting apart") cause the artistic, ritual and devotional mediations employed by Catholics to appear ridiculous to the Protestant by comparison and suggest to him that the Catholic does not recognize God as God, that he worships an idol in His place, that he offends against the honor due to God alone and that he attempts to enslave God by means of a series of magical procedures.

Protestantism was born from a revolt against clerics. This has left a lasting mark. It is not acceptable for a group distinct from the community and holding powers given from on high to intervene between the faithful and God. The idea of a universal priesthood of the baptized is expressed in detestation of Catholic clericalism. Or, if clericalism in the Catholic Church is considered to be a deviation from legitimate hierarchy, a sickness affecting the ecclesiastical body, then it is hard to see how priests would be able to rid themselves of it completely and definitively, given the reality of human nature. Such a thing has never been seen. Even though the Catholic world has been undergoing a general shrinking for two centuries, the clerical patient shows no sign of healing, and the illness may even be getting more acute as the flock becomes smaller and the Church turns into a sect. To be sure, clerical ways can be found just as much, and sometimes more, among Protestant pastors. But the Protestant community knows that its clerics come from within, whether, with the Lutherans, they are designated by natural authorities, or, with the Calvinists, a consensus of the people is necessary and officially required. Luther, and following him all Protestantism, rejects the Catholic doctrine according to which the ministerial priesthood is something added to the priesthood shared by the baptized. The Catholic priest appears as a man apart, marked by the sacrament of the order and endowed with powers that the lay person cannot exercise. Throughout all of Protestantism, communion with God is the work of the Spirit and comes about by faith. Every person is a priest for himself, because he has direct access to God and to Christ and has no need of an intermediary. Every member is authorized to perform the acts of worship and to fulfill ecclesiastical functions. In the radical Reformation, ministers are rejected and communities have no pastors (Gounelle). In the Calvinist Reformation, specialized ministers are held to be necessary, not for theological but simply for practical reasons. They perform as minister, but not as magisterium. They look toward God and toward the community that publically recognizes their vocation. Because of these dispositions of Protestantism, the idea of hierarchy, a theological idea as old as Christianity, is hidden behind Catholic clericalism and the Roman hierarchy that is its illegitimate double, but the only one that can be seen "from outside."

The priesthood of all believers, free inquiry, and the individual, learned, interpretive reading of the Bible together give the Protestant a very strong feeling of freedom—and, concerning Catholicism, of liberation.

The Catholic Church has *dogmas*. The dogmas are considered to be guides for the understanding of faith, and even guides for the mind simply. Faith claims to liberate us from intelligence, but faith is explained, channeled and defined by dogmas that achieve this liberation by bringing "errors" to an end. It must be acknowledged that, throughout intellectual history, it has often happened that they have acted as limits rather than beacons. Protestantism in almost all its varieties may profess the original symbols of the faith (the creeds of Nicaea, Constantinople, and Athanasia), but it refuses to recognize that it too has dogmas. It wants to have only *principles*, of which there are two: the "formal" principle of the sovereign authority of Scripture and the "material" principle of justification by grace (or by faith). Protestantism can crumble into thirty, one hundred, or two hundred different "denominations." The fragmentation happens at the level of doctrines that spring from free and contradictory interpretations of Scripture, which can be read a thousand ways. But the unity of Protestantism is guaranteed by the confession of these two principles upon which all the denominations are in agreement.

The result is a profoundly individual religion, one that is only truly religious when an individual soul makes it its own. The Princess of the Palatine, who remained Calvinist in the depths of her heart, explained to a lady of the court that "here [the Palatinate] everyone makes his own little religion." This statement shows how hateful was any moral constraint or religious education that might tend to stifle the personality. The success of Rousseau's pedagogical ideas is thus understandable. Even though they were founded on a humanistic optimism quite remote from the exasperated Augustinianism of Calvinism, they had the advantage of rejecting any effort to enclose the soul of the child in a mold. Protestant intolerance toward Catholicism, which caused Catholics to be emancipated much later in England, Sweden, Denmark, and Prussia much later than Protestants were in many Catholic countries (including France), resulted from an intense fear, sometimes turning to fanaticism, of a confessional constraint that might compromise the freedom necessary to a personal, conscious and thoughtful approach to religion. No tolerance for the enemies of tolerance! The only religion of worth is one that the individual gives himself. To worship "in spirit and truth" necessarily implies freedom of conscience, and the two formulas have the same content.

This carries over from religious to intellectual life. The Protestant world maintains a prejudice according to which the Catholic suffers from a mental handicap for the sole reason that he adheres to dogmas imposed from above or from outside, or in any case of which he is not the author. The great Theodor Mommsen (1817–1903) did not want Catholics named to university chairs, because their intellectual freedom and commitment to science was mutilated in advance by a belief that was not free. Mommsen was a liberal, and it was in the name of liberalism that he excluded Catholics. In Wilhelmian Prussia, if a person wanted to be a professor, it was almost better to be a Jew than a Catholic. In England there are plenty of brilliant thinkers who heap the bitterest sarcasms on Christianity in general. But when it comes to Catholicism, they become angry and wonder how such a failure of intelligence is possible and how this belief can attract any minds other than those already very far gone in cretinism.

The emphasis on the personal nature of every religious act explains the persistence of Protestant unease concerning infant baptism, which reaches its height in the Baptist movement. This is why it sets up a ceremony called "confirmation" or "reception of catechumens" and delays it almost to the age of adulthood. It is only at this age that the child can truly, in full personal responsibility, give himself to God and to Jesus Christ. From this point of view the early communion of Catholics reflects a magical conception of the sacrament as a kind of "lucky charm." Prayer must be so personal that formulaic prayers are distrusted, and this includes the recitation of the Lord's Prayer, for any fixed text detracts from sincere and responsible commitment and risks degenerating into mere verbalism. Even the sign of the cross is suppressed, though it contains a baptismal formula accepted by all Protestants.

The process of internalizing faith, by which the believer commits himself more and more profoundly following his initial act of conversion, a process that causes him increasingly to despise every pre-set gesture or imposed behavior, continues to be experienced as an act of freedom. The establishment of Calvinism, especially in New England, at first had the character of an almost theocratic control and of a stifling official moralism. But as the sense of duty was gradually internalized, this control was no longer necessary; as constraint sank deeper into the soul it inscribed itself in the conscience as an immaterial, intangible and sacred principle, until control was able to disappear and give way to the most liberal forms of democracy. Montesquieu wrote that the mainspring of the republican form of government is virtue; he might have observed how tight this spring was in the little states of the East Coast and how it levelled the paths of democratization. The authoritarianism of the Calvinist city disappears in favor of the free responsibility of each of its members. And this is why, when there is a revolt against Puritan constraint, it first takes the form of attacking what is most intimate in it: sexual reserve, abstinence, bodily cleanliness, and decency in attire. It is rare that it goes back to the political forms that guarantee freedom. But it is rarer still that it lasts very long, and the moral reaction unfailingly restores the old order, as if to prove that one may violate the moral system, but never break free of it (Bouyer). Updike (after Lawrence, Miller, and a thousand others) has marvelously described this systole and diastole of the American heart. The re-establishment proceeds in reverse order and begins with sex, alcohol, and tobacco.

Why does one remain Protestant? We have tried to enumerate the reasons. Some are found in external conditioning: the existing order of politics, heredity, and custom. Others are more internal, but still external to religion, such as fidelity to the community, national honor and patriotism. To these can be added a feeling of revolt, which, moreover, may be shared with the Catholic, against all forms of clericalism. Finally there is a noble attachment to personal freedom and responsibility. These are the negative reasons that divide the Protestant from the dominant Catholicism. But the positive reason is something we can access only by entering more profoundly into Protestant spirituality. For Protestantism would not have "held on" if it had not been able to fulfill the Christian souls of its adepts and to satisfy their spiritual needs sufficiently that they did not need to inquire into the Catholic religion, that they remained deaf to Catholic appeals for unity, and that they did not suffer from the famous "variations" for which Bossuet reproached them. "It pleases us, sir," Leibniz answered, "to be of this Church which is in motion and variable" (Gagnebin).

Anabaptism

Now I must go backwards. The end of this essay, I must remind the reader, will deal with the new religious formations that are called evangelical and that derive mainly from the Baptist movement and from Pentecostalism.

The Baptists have a prehistory. They are convinced that their principles go back to the origins of Christianity. They are heirs of Anabaptism.

To grasp the spirit of the Baptist movement one must consider its vision of history from the beginnings of the Christian religion, of which the Baptists believe they are the faithful branch. I will follow Georges Rousseau, a Baptist pastor, who offers a clear and vigorous synthesis.

In the beginning, when Jesus Christ founded the church, there was no established priesthood, despite the way the body of apostles is presented. In the beginning is the believing community, a community of men and women born into the life of the spirit, confessing the same faith, united in the same baptism, detached from the world. These churches are open to all those who agree to enlist themselves under the orders of their Lord and to wear the sign of the Christ. United with his Savior, the sinner, forgiven and justified, enters into the new life of holiness inspired by the Spirit of God, against which the Adversary fights.

The first churches were on the margins of the world and constituted a foreign and unassimilable body, as appropriate to their divine vocation to be true witnesses even unto martyrdom. Their practices of worship were simple and devoid of splendor. The rite of initiation was baptism, administered by immersion. It signified a symbolic act of faithfulness, and also a confession of faith involving the commitment of one's whole life. This was a birth from On High, according to the Spirit, because the church was founded, not on any familial or racial bond, but on an individual union of the soul with God, through Christ. The other practice was the breaking of bread, first an "agape" or feast; then, little by little there arose distinct fraternal meals celebrating the Last Supper, a sharing among disciples of the symbols of the body and blood of Christ.

Each local community is the Church of Christ in an absolute sense. Each is the model or the example of the universal Church. Most separate themselves from Judaism. Peter, John, and James are the first leaders of these Churches, without however exercising the authority of a clerical office. Christ the Lord is the only head.

Nevertheless, these Churches, as they abandon a primitive communism, must organize themselves. The principle accepted by all was that every function in the Church was exercised by virtue of a vocation from God, a gift of grace by the Spirit, that this function must make manifest. The elected functions are those of presbyters, elders, and deacons. There are also charismatic ministers, but without any trace of a hierarchy or even a line dividing clerics from lay members. The local Churches are autonomous, independent, and united only in faith.

Unfortunately, in the post-apostolic period, signs of degeneration began to corrupt the beautiful original idea. Initiation rites that had been simple symbols of inner grace began imperceptibly to be considered as conferring this grace. This was a return either to the practice of pagan mysteries or to the legalistic ritualism of pharisaic Judaism. Those who presided over these rights constituted a class apart, the *sacerdotes*. New notions appeared: sacraments, a priestly class, a holy universal church, a visible power, at once political and religious. The idea of a sacrament altered the very foundation of the Christian religion, that is, personal faith that justifies and saves the sinner. And if sacraments are necessary to salvation, a clergy becomes indispensable as the basis of the Church's authority and power. As long as baptism is a symbol, one might if need be do without it. But if it becomes a sacrament, and if immersion is difficult to practice, then sprinkling suffices, because, rather than a symbol, baptism is now identified with what is symbolized, namely regeneration. Given the new meaning of baptism and the fear of perdition, the sick and eventually infants are baptized, lest they die before being regenerated by the sacrament. In the same way, the idea of sacramental grace deformed and corrupted the Holy Supper. It became a sacrifice effectively offered to God, a vain repetition of the unique sacrifice of the Cross. Finally, following the example of the Old Testament, the training of an ordained clergy changed the nature of ministers in the Church, and once they had assumed a monopoly of the administration of the sacraments, all charismatic ministries disappeared from Christian congregations.

Such a disastrous deformation had to provoke resistance on the part of those who remembered the primitive church. Monasticism was an early reaction, one unfortunately spoiled by a useless asceticism, which led to the exaltation of chastity and then to the worship of Mary and to the appearance of the sacrament of penitence.

Montanism and Novatianism can also be considered legitimate forms of protest. Donatism deserves respect for its concern for the purity of Churches. The dominant Church applied the term "heretic" to these movements, and when the Roman emperors became Christian, they applied temporal power to their forcible repression. Thus began the persecutions. But they were not able to stamp out the revolts of conscience against the abandonment of the apostolic idea. These persecutions make up a long chain in the "time of shame," which includes the Joachimites, Savonarola, and Wycliffe. Among their early witnesses the Baptists recognize Berengar of Tours (d. 1088), who attacked the received doctrine of baptism and proclaimed that the few who did not bow before the error were the true Church; Peter of Bruis (burned alive in 1126), an Anabaptist before the letter who practiced "re-baptism" at the age of adult conscience; and Henry of Lausanne (d. 1147). Baptists also honor, as elder brothers, the Bohemian church of the United Brethren, the Taborites, Wycliffe, and Jan Hus.

An examination of this historical sketch begins to clarify the physiognomy of the Baptist movement. There is a decided refusal of ecclesiastical institutions, that is, those of the Catholic Church up to the Reformation, and then those of established Protestantism. There is a notable insistence on the personal commitment of the act of faith, which obliterates the realism of the sacraments in favor of a rigorously symbolic interpretation. This leads to a fraternal sympathy for various "heresies," insofar as these were persecuted for holding comparable positions. Finally, there is a penchant or taste for separation from the world, and in particular from the state, that produces a spirit of sectarianism that does not shrink before a limitless scissiparity, justified by the total independence of each community from all the others. Let us now see how the Baptist movement set itself apart within the Reformation.

Anabaptism proper seems to have been born within the Zwinglian movement. Zwingli himself was for a time practically an Anabaptist, by virtue of the fact that, according to him, Scripture said nothing in favor of the baptism of infants.

The thesis of the "rebaptizers" was that infant baptism bound together indissolubly Church and State. In fact the principle of union of the Church with the State cannot exist unless all children are baptized at birth, so that a country's population can be religiously homogeneous, without regard to the personal faith of inhabitants. In the eyes of the established Churches, the fight against "pedobaptism" symbolizes the cause of the complete separation of the Church from the State. Anabaptism thus represents the radical wing of the Reformation, whose other principles it accepts, namely: the authority of holy Scripture as superior to that of the tradition; the sole Lordship of Christ in the personal life of the Christian, without the interference of a pre-existing hierarchical power, religious or civil; spirituality as essential to the faith, and as disqualifying the sacerdotal hierarchy and its rites; the freedom and equality of believers, responsible before God alone, or before a governing power that they have chosen freely according to the dictates of Scripture; the spiritual nature of the church as a free community of believers, inwardly renewed by the Holy Spirit and determined to live as disciples of Christ; and independence from the state for the free management of the affairs of the religious community. In all this the refusal of infant baptism is considered the test and the keystone.

Nevertheless, Zwingli had to hold things together. The members of the town Council of Zürich had been baptized as infants and thus considered themselves rightful members of the church they were organizing along with Zwingli. They did not see the need to go through a personal conversion or a new baptism of faith. Beginning in 1523 it was in fact a state church that was established and that took over the religious education of children regularly baptized at birth. At this time a group of "brethren," led by Grebel, a disciple of Zwingli, broke off. The new community proclaimed the primacy of faith and of spiritual and personal experience, from which a new church was supposed to arise, one that was truly reformed, in conformity with the gospel, with the local community as its base, and soon a new state in conformity with gospel norms. "One must obey God rather than men," said St. Peter. But "men" put Grebel in prison, where he died, and burned his associates at the stake, or threw them in a Zürich lake, in order to teach them about re-baptism! After this there was no end to the persecution.

We hear little of the massacre of the Anabaptists, because they were persecuted both by Protestants and by Catholics, who preserved the memory of their respective martyrs and had no pity for these dangerous revolutionaries who put the common political order in danger. The extermination is nevertheless remarkable even by the standard of the customs of the era. The Baptist movement spread like wildfire, to the south in the direction of Tyrol, to the east, along the Danube and through the Rhine valley, and to the north, to Alsace and the Low Countries. In the 1530, its presence is noted in Scandinavia and in England. An imperial mandate of 1528, which became the edict of the Empire to the Diet of Spire in 1529, destined all Anabaptists to "death by fire, sword or any other means without any prior inquisitorial justice." The theologian Hubmaier, after some careful torture, was burned and his wife thrown in the Danube with a stone around her neck. Another theologian, Sattler, codified congregationalism in 1527. One enters the Church, he explains, by the baptism of faith. The Holy Supper is a manifestation of spiritual unity in Christ. Autonomous assemblies choose their pastors and deacons; these assemblies may form groups. The only disciplinary sanction is excommunication. The world and its ways must be rejected. The State is a necessary evil and Christians have no place in it. These principles remain fundamental for constitutions used by Congregationalists, Baptists and Quakers. The did not prevent—quite the contrary—Sattler from being tortured with red-hot pincers, having his tongue cut out, or from going to the stake while his wife was thrown in the Neckar for following him.

Seen as a whole, Anabaptism was a spiritual Protestantism, born along with the Reformation and often heir of earlier movements. Geographically it forms a kind of crescent, from the Rhine valley to the Danube valley, extending to Hungary, Transylvania and Lithuania, a kind of buffer zone between Lutheran Germany and Calvinist Western Europe. It is more a state of mind of piety, congregationalist organization and resistance to authorities than an articulate theological doctrine. In the world of the peasants and craftsmen where it took hold, theology was not a high priority. It should be recalled, however, that the oldest of the Reformed professions of faith, that of Schleitheim in 1527, preceded the Augsburg Confession by two years. There we find the rejection of the state (which Luther, for his part, reveres), the extreme relativizing of the sacraments and the rigorous distinction between the elect and the damned, saints and sinners. This is why excommunication is an essential element of their discipline.

By its own momentum, and spurred on by persecution, the Anabaptist movement, the left wing of the Reformation, rapidly radicalized. Among the common people it combined with a millenarianism that had been smoldering since the thirteenth century without ever being extinguished. Thomas Müntzer, the self-styled "sword of Gideon," was not exactly an Anabaptist, but he was taken for one. The huge peasant revolt that he ended up leading was defeated in 1525 under the curses of Luther and the boots of knights. Even after this crushing defeat, millenarianism remained active in Switzerland and the Low Countries. The most famous episode is that of Münster, where the communist regime of Jean de Leyde sustained a siege of sixteen months against the imperial troops, both Catholic and Protestant (1535). The taking of the city marked the movement's decline. Repression spread throughout Europe and produced perhaps a hundred thousand victims. Calvin, having failed to lay hands on an Anabaptist who infected Geneva by his presence, and learning that he had taken refuge in Valencia, Spain, wrote to warn the local Catholic Inquisition of the danger. Few books of martyrs are as well supplied as those of the Anabaptists and Baptists. Their bad reputation has held up over centuries.

Voltaire, in *Candide*, transposes the parable of the Good Samaritan to a Dutch Anabaptist, surrounded by universal disdain, who alone cares for the agonizing Pangloss. In his *English Letters*, another Baptist is the only decent Christian.

Here it might be permissible to interject a melancholy reflection. Essentially, if one is willing to set aside the chiliasm that made them such an object of fear at their beginning, the Anabaptists demanded the radical separation of Church and State, complete religious freedom, and individual conversion as the sign of Christian identity. The first item was secured in France in 1905, the second by the whole Catholic Church during Vatican II, and the third has been more and more clearly demanded since 1968. These demands also included the abolition of the clergy, which happened all by itself due to the rapid decline of ecclesiastical recruitment. Finally there is the suppression of infant baptism. This practice is making its way with the progress of the ideology of democratic human rights, which raises concerns about infringing upon the freedom of minors. The Catholic Church, moreover, under the influence of socialism and especially communism, has not been exempt in the twentieth century from the infiltration of millenarianism, from which the Baptists quickly removed themselves in the eighteenth century, but which was awakened in the Church in forms analogous to Anabaptism. In many places Catholics are not equipped to answer Baptists, whose faith and missionary ardor are at least equal to their own, with arguments drawn from a more adequate theology. It is understandable that they offer little resistance to Baptist competition in Latin America, which has been a fertile soil for liberation theology, or in Africa, for other reasons, especially since they are themselves more Baptist than they know.

After the slaughter, the Anabaptist movement settled down, and, under the influence of a man of moderation, the Dutch Menno Simmons, it abandoned its apocalyptic views and retreated to the simple practice of the Evangelical life. We will not follow the Mennonite progeny, which still exists in the form of tight, peaceful, nonproselytizing communities, including the Amish, who now make up a picturesque part of the American landscape. Nor will we trace the anti-Trinitarian current that is also linked to Anabaptism, nor its multiple offshoots in Italy, Poland, Spain, Switzerland (where, as we know, Servetus played a major role, along with Calvin), and elsewhere.

We now leave aside the history of European Protestantism. From this point on we will go over to England, then to America, since it is from the Anglo-Saxon world that Protestantism now draws its vitality.

III.
England

Anglicanism

We will not look at Anglicanism in itself, but only in relation with the world of the Reformation and its American offshoots. Still, a sketch is necessary.

There is a feature that stands out at once: for the first time, the religious revolution arises in the context of a great unified state and under the control of the state. The ebb and flow of this revolution, which will last almost two centuries before reaching definitive stability, will take place in the rigorous framework of a changing legal order; it is relentless, but always under the law. The second feature is that doctrinal evolution is subject to the political necessity of supporting the unity of the kingdom in obedience and uniformity. This is why the directly doctrinal aspects are generally veiled, or express themselves in a politically conditioned way, in ambiguous formulations, in order to take account of the balance of power and of the real diversity of convictions that lies beneath the uniformity of texts imposed on all.

England is a small and little populated country but, beginning in the fifteenth century, one of the richest and most highly educated in Europe. For this reason the religious movement was not limited to the clerical world. There was competition between the culture and the ecclesiastical culture. Humanism is flourishing brilliantly, and it is a more pious humanism than in Italy; its main voices are men of the Church or close to the Church (Colet, Linacre, Fisher, More), and all discuss the Bible as a primary reference. Personal faith is expected; the *devotion moderna* found this country to be an essential base.

The institutional church is proportionately more powerful than in France. It possesses a good fifth of national wealth and its income is more than twice that of the Crown. England, which has hardly more than two and a half million inhabitants, can spread across the landscape powerful abbeys and cathedrals even more immense than the French. Among the middle class, anticlericalism develops as a counter-influence, as is normal. Wycliffe, the inspiration of the Lollards and of Jan Hus, expresses already at the end of the fourteenth century a number of future themes besides the usual denunciation of Church abuses, calling for the Crown's intervention to limit the Church; he also translates the Bible, contests pontifical authority and, finally, refuses to recognize the Real Presence in the Eucharist. Wycliffe's writings were distributed only in manuscript form. They were followed by the gradual arrival of Lutheran theses, first in universities, then slowly in commercial circles in the Southeast, which was in touch with continental affairs.

There thus exists a reform movement in the English Church, as throughout the Catholic Church in this period. It is not particularly virulent. As in France, the Church had taken its distance from a Rome much weakened by the Great Schism. Anglicanism might very well have gone no further than French Gallicanism. Henry Tudor was a brilliant king, a humanist named "defender of the faith" by the pope, still more absolute than Francis I, holding the clergy solidly in his hand, admired by cultivated elites, close to a still fundamentally Catholic people; he might have been content with the kind of limited control exercised by the French king. But it so happened that he needed papal authorization on a particular point, and that brought everything down.

Henry VIII wanted a male heir that his wife Catherine of Aragon could not give him. And he was in love with Anne Boleyn. He needed the pope to annul his marriage. The king, who was pious and a good theologian, could invoke a prohibition from Leviticus. Each step in the process was communicated to all of Europe. The University of Paris approved the king's point of view, and Luther, the queen's. But judgment rested in the pope's hands. Anne became pregnant and the king secretly married her. But how was this to be made legitimate? This was a job for Cranmer, who had been made Archbishop of Canterbury in 1533. With the support of the Convocation of the clergy, he declared the first marriage null and void and validated the second; Anne was crowned at Westminster. Soon came excommunication, and the schism was consummated.

From here everything went very fast. The king made this a test of his absolute power, with the help of Cranmer and of the layman Thomas Cromwell, "vicar-general" of ecclesiastical affairs. The Convocations gave him the title of "supreme head" of the Church "so far as the law of Christ allows" and entrusted him with the care of souls. The pope was henceforth referred to as "Bishop of Rome." The Supremacy Act of 1534 legalized the king's title as "the only Supreme head on Earth of the Church in England," with no restrictive clause. In 1535 began the first terror that struck the Church; the second came under Mary Tudor and the third under Elizabeth. Thomas More, the Chancellor of England, put his head on the block. Monks who refused to swear the oath of supremacy were put to death. Monasteries were dissolved, and the abbots of famous abbeys in Glastonbury, Reading, and Colchester were hanged. In the north rebels were hanged or, like traitors, castrated, eviscerated and quartered.

On the whole the English people were brought to submission. Obedience to civil power was well established. National feeling condemned dissidence. Rome had not released the English from their duty of obedience, nor had it permitted them to rebel. There were cases of passive resistance. Thomas More's took place in a judicial context: the new statutes contradict the laws of God. To force subjects to support statutes when their representatives (the Parliament) were denied the right to discussion is an abuse of power. There were also cases of armed resistance, most notably that of the Pilgrimage of Grace that broke out in Lincolnshire and Yorkshire. It was crushed mercilessly and without much difficulty. Cardinal Pole sought for help from Charles V, Francois I, and Pope Paul III. The first two pushed back against these efforts as they were able, and Paul III finally provided a bull of excommunication, but much too late. His power was blunted, and Henry VIII remained master of his kingdom.

Protestantism came out more into the open with the schism, and the king, fearing the Catholic union between Francis I and Charles V, made contact with the Lutherans and with Melanchthon. The plan presented by the latter was refused. Still these talks resulted in the confession known as the Ten Articles, the least Catholic of Henry's reign. It mentions three sacraments, but does not deny the existence of others. It affirms the real presence, but without referring to transubstantiation. It does not mention justification by faith alone and recommends masses and prayers for the deceased.

Three years later, in 1539, Catherine of Aragon having died and Melanchthon having been dismissed, the king was able to impose "An Act Abolishing Diversity in Opinions," which soon came to be known as "the bloody whip with six strings," which clearly affirmed transubstantiation, the celibacy of secular priests, monastic vows, private masses, etc.—in short, an intransigent doctrinal Catholicism, a disaster for the Reformers at the end of Henry's reign. To deny transubstantiation exposed one to the stake. A third Confession of Faith, in 1543, pushed the Catholic reaction and royal supremacy to the last degree.

The reforming party was not dead, however, and the king's two main collaborators were more or less openly part of it. Thomas Cromwell sponsored the great Bible in English of 1539 and packed the episcopate with reformers. The rich figure of Cranmer is more beautiful and more complex than that of this brutal executor. As Archbishop of Canterbury he had secretly espoused the daughter of the Lutheran German Osiander and had had her brought to England in a trunk. He found it wise to send her back temporarily to Germany in the last years of the reign. His religious genius was great and profound, and his liturgical sense exceptional, but he evolved gradually in a Lutheran direction. He loved the king, who also loved him and called him to his bedside during his terrible agony.

Edward VI was only nine years old at the time of his accession (1547). Intelligent and pious, he had been educated by strict Calvinists, among them the famous John Knox, the Scottish reformer, who became his chaplain.

The first measure was that the crown could depose as it wished prelates who displeased it, which is pure Erastianism. The second, more important measure was liturgical reform, whose architect was Cranmer. This was conducted with consummate skill, proceeding mainly by omissions, the Protestant meaning of which usually remained hidden to the faithful. It was permitted to replace auricular confession with general confession. Candelmas, Ash Wednesday, and Palm Sunday were dropped. In London services were now held in English. Most important, on 21 January 1549 there appeared the *Book of Common Prayer*, also called the *Prayer Book*, which was required by the Act of Uniformity, and which became the authoritative cornerstone of Anglicanism.

According to the Ordinal, which fixed the rights of the ordination of clergy, the priest was no longer the minister of a sacrifice, but the minister of the Word and the dispenser of sacraments. Protesting bishops were sent to the tower, and one of the replacement bishops, John Hopper, named to the seat of Gloucester, refused to wear the prescribed liturgical vestments. The Puritans came to consider him the father of non-conformism. The new version of the Prayer Book in 1552 pushed the Protestant tendency further. It no longer contains "the rites and ceremonies of the Church," but only the "worship" of the church of England. The terms "mass," "altar," and "sacrifice" are omitted. The words of the minister who distributes the communion affirm that it is a simple remembrance, in conformity with the doctrine of Zwingli. The rest follows: the suppression of the Reservation of the Eucharist, of the practice of taking the communion to the sick, of prayers for the deceased, etc. An additional commentary, called the *Black Rubric*, forbad any Catholic-leaning interpretation of the *Prayer Book*, as had still been possible in the first edition.

Cranmer's work was crowned by the publication of the *Forty-Two Articles of Religion*. This was again a compromise between the two extremes of Catholicism and of a Baptist Calvinism. It takes justification by faith alone from Luther, predestination from Calvin, and the rejection of the real presence from Zwingli. The Catholic theses of the sacrificial mass, transubstantiation, the *ex opera operato* efficacy of the sacraments, purgatory, and the cult of saints are expressly rejected, along with the primacy of Rome, the infallibility of ecumenical councils and obligatory ecclesiastical celibacy. This declaration of the *Forty-Two Articles* marked the high tide of Protestantism. It would never be surpassed. But it provided the basis of the Elizabethan *Thirty-Nine Articles* of 1563.

It would be hard to find a more abrupt change of course than that which marked the short reign (1553–1558) of the daughter of Henry VIII and Catherine of Aragon. Mary Tudor's first act was to abolish her predecessor's religious legislation, to release from prison and reinstate the Catholic bishops, to restore the mass, and finally to suppress the *Prayer Book*. The Catholic restoration was complete. It remained to reconcile with Rome, which was done under the aegis of the Pope's legate, Cardinal Pole.

Bloody Mary's terror was in no way inferior to what had happened under her father. The difference was that the martyrs of her reign were piously preserved and venerated more than the martyrs of other reigns. Almost 300 Protestants were burned, clerics and laymen, men and women. Cranmer was torn between his faith and his loyalty to royal supremacy; at first he submitted. But when he was nevertheless tortured, he reached toward the fire with the hand that had signed his abjurations. He then wrote a very beautiful prayer that concludes as follows: "have mercy upon me, O God! Whose property is always to have mercy. My sins are great: but Thy mercy is still greater. —Oh Lord, for Christ's sake, hear me— hear me most gracious God!"

It seems not to have been the question of faith that outraged the English people. In the end, they did not like changes in their parishes, and higher authorities, whose intentions were more definite, had labored rather to cushion the blows. But it was a case of national feeling. The drama surrounding Mary Tudor was her marriage. Her union with Prince Philip of Spain, the son of Charles

V, whose heir she failed to produce, was experienced vaguely as a treason. The pointless ferocity of her repression meant that the English people associated three things that might have remained separated: Catholicism, the specter of foreign domination (that of the detested Spain united with Rome), and religious fanaticism. There could be no more question of a pure and simple return to Catholicism after the death of Mary Tudor.

Henry, Edward, and Mary were devout Christians and even good theologians. Elizabeth was neither in the slightest. She was guided by political reason in these matters. The middle way that she chose corresponded exactly to the balance of power and situated itself in religious England's center of gravity. The country that had changed religions three times in 25 years, passing from a Catholicism without Pope to Protestantism and then to an intransigent Catholicism, always by Royal decision, was tired and ripe for compromise. From the moment of her coronation, from her first steps, the Queen showed that she was master. Theologically she took her distance from the hard-core Knox, and took her bearings instead from more moderate ideas. Then she had the Commons approve the two fundamental laws of Anglicanism. The Act of Supremacy abolished the laws of the preceding reign and made the Queen "the sole supreme governor" of the realm. The word was "governor" and no longer "head," as under Henry VIII: the Queen therefore exercised only a "jurisdictional power" over the church and not an "ordering power." Thus a certain spiritual autonomy was preserved. An oath of obedience to the crown in religious matters was imposed on the clergy as on all state employees. The Uniformity Act, which passed with a small majority, brought back the *Prayer Book*, in a slightly more Protestant version than that of 1549 and slightly less than that of 1552. The Black Rubric, which had introduced inconvenient theological precision in the book, was omitted, and liturgical vestments were reestablished. Nevertheless, all the Catholic bishops (named by Mary Tudor) except for one refused to swear the oath of obedience to the act of supremacy. They were deposed, some were imprisoned, and then replaced. The Protestant Matthew Parker occupied the seat of Canterbury. The 39 articles of religion (1563) were written in such a way that some articles might be interpreted in different ways. Still in 1836, Newman's Tract 90 claimed to show that these articles were consistent with a Catholic interpretation.

Elizabeth managed Catholics carefully, believing that they would eventually come to her side and recognize her full legitimacy. She received unexpected help from Philip II, former husband of Mary Tudor, who had big plans for an alliance with England against France. He held back the hand of the Pope, who was ready to pronounce excommunication. But Pope Pius V, the militant Pope of the Council of Trent, believed that England was on the verge of a general uprising: in February 1570 the bull *Regnans in excelsis*, which excommunicated the Queen, was handed down. From this moment the recusants fell subject to supreme punishment and the martyrs multiplied. Mary Stuart, the hope of the Catholics, was executed in 1587. Philip II had changed politics and now wanted to have done with this heretical and predatory kingdom. The Pope supported him imprudently. The defeat of the Invincible Armada (1588) and the intense patriotic reaction that followed sealed the fate of English Catholics. For centuries they were considered traitors and outlaws.

Considering the central role of the state in England's religious evolution, as well as all the blood that had been spilt, for the most part legally, but without mercy, one might expect Christianity in England to have become a desiccated and closely monitored state religion reduced to an obligatory ritualism.

This was not at all the case. Subject to fines, under the Uniformity Act all the Queen's subjects were obligated to attend Sunday services. And so they did, *Prayer Book* in hand. Theologically they might find there a doctrine of the Eucharist that was very close to the strictest Zwinglianism. Despite relentlessly equivocal formulas, it is clear that the sacrificial aspects had been evacuated and that the communion meant nothing more than a commitment to a life illuminated by the Gospel (Bouyer). While the mass is gravely emptied of its meaning, though still properly celebrated, there remain the Morning and Evening (vespers) Prayers, where the liturgical ge-nius of Cranmer is at its best. They are very dependent upon the Catholic breviary. Cranmer also introduced what was most pre-cious in the monastic tradition, the complete recitation of the Psalter, the morning *Te Deum* and *Benedictus* and the evening *Magnificat* and *Nunc Dimittis*, enhanced by the most beautiful prayers. The extraordinary majesty of the English liturgical lan-guage succeeds in giving these services a sense of the sacred and an educative value that satisfy the spiritual needs of the people. The veil deliberately placed over theological disputation allowed the English people to live by the ancient adage: *Lex orandi, lex cre-dendi* (one believes as one worships). The perfectly orthodox law of prayer sets the tone for the faith. The simple believer is not re-quired to swear allegiance to the 39 Articles of Religion; only the clergy is subject to it.

Moreover, as we have already emphasized, there is in the king-dom a very lively lay culture and a Christian humanism capable of independent thought. Thus, over a whole century, there were elite minds capable of "breathing a soul into the Elizabethan compro-mise." Hooker's *Laws of Ecclesiastic Polity* has the breadth and often the quality of the great medieval summas. Some consider its author the Saint Thomas Aquinas of Anglicanism. The three points that remain fundamental to this church's tradition and opposed to Calvinism are, first the constant reference to the Fathers of the era of Constantine. Next there is the firm rejection of the Ockhamist concept of *potentia absoluta*: all divine law finds its principle, not in the arbitrary and unknowable will of God alone, but in the iden-tity of the will of God with infinite reason. God acts according to His wisdom. Finally, the Church is not only a free association of believers, or a society built on an imagined New Testament model. Contrary to the teachings of Zwingli and Calvin, it is an historical body that grows organically. On these there points Hooker is Catholic.

Under the reigns that followed, Anglican orthodoxy took shape and experienced its Golden age. The greatness of the language of the King James Bible (1611) has no rival except perhaps in Luther's

Bible. In this era it takes its place in the English language, as well as in its literature and spirituality. John Donne, along with Herbert, Vaughan, Traherne, and Crashaw make up the great company of "metaphysical" poets. The theologians of Charles I, the Caroline Divines, and in particular, the first among them, Lancelot Andrews, always drawing upon the Greek fathers, in many respects (notably the doctrine of real presence) return to Catholic orthodoxy.

Anglicanism is thus a learned religion, rich in patristic and humanistic culture. It is a living religion, whose piety finds expression in poetry and in an abundant and profound hymnody that does not hesitate to borrow from Continental authors of all confessions. By instinct and a pragmatism that avoids endangering the country's unity it avoids definitions that are too precise. It declares itself catholic. The old popular and parochial depths of the country is thus reassured, since the form of worship has been changed not by additions, but essentially by omissions, which shock less. The church is proud of never having been reformed (or so it thinks). It has had neither its Luther, nor its Calvin, nor its Council of Trent. It considers itself as a continuation without rupture of the ancient Church. In religion as in politics England makes a revolution by going back, as if by a return to a past order that had been transgressed. It sees itself as a bridge between Protestantism and the Roman Church.

In short, Anglicanism takes part in English "freedom." But the gray areas, the lack of doctrinal precision, result in a kind of latent breakdown of the Church. A rationalist current appears as early as the seventeenth century, especially at Cambridge and among those known as the Cambridge Platonists. This was the origin of the "latitudinarians," the liberals, of the Broad Church and the Low Church movements where Protestant influences find refuge. The High Church is more conservative politically, liturgically and theologically. These diverse currents may erode the unity of the Church, but they do not destroy it, for the principle of unity moves from the faith toward the political community. On the one hand, the Anglican Church, in its piety, its hymns, and its admirable liturgy rightly prides itself in its "glorious comprehensiveness." On the other hand, it is only one of the more beautiful of England's institutions. Seen from this angle, it sometimes seems that its prayer, its praise, and its incense go up not to God alone, but also, inseparably, to England and to the set of values gathered in this word. Newman saw it as a great human creation:

"I recognize in the Anglican Church a time-honored institution, of noble historical memories, a monument of ancient wisdom, a momentous arm of political strength, a great national organ, a source of vast popular advantage, and, to a certain point, a witness and teacher of religious truth."

But this was not enough to satisfy Catholics, with their concern for the universality and independence of the Church and for a confession of faith *ne varietur*. Nor did it satisfy Protestants, of whom we will now speak.

The Puritans

The word "puritanism" appears in the middle of the seventeenth century. It does not designate a doctrine, but rather a state of mind that is at once religious and political. Richard Baxter, at the end of this century, notes that "any person inclined toward a serious conception of religion (even with a moderate hierarchy and liturgy) was considered to be a Puritan if he lived in accordance with professed principles." Baxter applies the term in the first instance to Presbyterians, that is to say Calvinists. But Strafford, advisor to Charles I, provides a political definition: "the very genius of this nation [the Puritans] leads it to oppose everything authority would impose on it in civil as well as in ecclesiastical matters." The spirit of religious seriousness is combined with a spirit of political defiance and of economic individualism. The Puritans retain elements of the Calvinist program, including the sanctification of existence in all its aspects—social, economic, and sexual. This is why Max Weber uses the term Puritan in the sense it had in the popular language of the seventeenth century, "when it designated the religious movements of Holland and of England that tended toward asceticism, whatever their church organization and their doctrine," thus including "Independents," Congregationalists, Baptists, Mennonites, and Quakers.

Puritanism thus has many layers: religious (according to the type of faith and of church organization), political, and moral. The unifying theme is the aspiration to purity and to simplicity and disgust for the conventions and vices of this world. There were still Catholics in England, and the Anglican Church, under the aegis of the state, called itself catholic, having simply returned to a condition prior to Roman corruptions. Puritanism thus represented the true spirit of the Reformation: authentic, spontaneous, fervent, and arising from the depths of the English people. It was capable of initiating the long secular process of the English revolution.

Puritanism cannot be identified with this revolution. We cannot speak of the Puritan revolution, because this vast movement, which extends from the 1640s until the beginning of the eighteenth century, goes beyond religion in so many ways. But Puritanism is at the point of departure of what English historians call, not the revolution, but "the great rebellion." The religious passion, Henri Hauser writes (citing Leonard),

> is not a religion of pure form, the attachment to a ritual or to a hierarchy, but religion conceived as an inward drama, a dialogue between the trembling human being and the sovereign God, a kind of cold and almost rationalist mysticism, a matter of conscience to which the Englishman brings the same spirit of seriousness, the same rigid and strict honesty, I would almost say the same rules of accounting that apply in business. [...] Puritanism still represented a spiritual attitude more than a credo or a party, not yet [under James I] an open hostility to the ecclesiastical hierarchy, but an obstinate attachment to the letter of Scripture, to worship in spirit and truth, a Calvinist disposition to consider everything that men have added to the word of God to be superfluous and often stained by papist idolatry.

With the coming of Elizabeth (1558), the reformed refugees hastened to return from Geneva. They sensed that persecution had come to an end. They hoped that England would at last be Protestant. How far would the Queen go? The Supremacy Act gave her all powers. The bishops that she put in place, in their hearts Protestants, wished at least to return to the principles of Edward VI, while hoping for more.

But the revision of the *Prayer Book* in 1552 contained much to worry the Reformed. It encouraged the reading of texts and thus restricted the role of the sermon and of the minister in the instruction of the faithful. The possibility of private communion was reintroduced, along with kneeling at the moment of communion and the use of a ring in the marriage ceremony. Respect for the saints' holidays was recommended. The litany that included prayer for deliverance from the Bishop of Rome and all his "detestable enormities" had disappeared. Ministers were supposed to wear the alb and chasuble. As this Vestiarian Controversy heated up it gave rise to the Puritan party. This party wished to require the black vestment of Geneva; it tried to pass its proposals in every session of Parliament. The queen cut off this argument by deciding that no religious legislation could be submitted to Parliament that had not received the prior consent of the bishops – whom she controlled.

King James I, who was Scottish and therefore in principle Calvinist, but son of the Catholic Mary Stuart, raised hopes in opposing camps. He disappointed both by continuing Elizabeth's policies. The Puritans submitted a respectful petition (signed by 1000 ministers) demanding the abolition of the practices noted above. The king convoked a council in which he actively participated, since he prided himself on theology. It came to nothing, except the imposition of the new translation of the Bible on all of England. This was the famous "authorized" version of 1611, a prodigious success, which not only transmitted the word of God but established a mystical link between England and Zion's election. But when the Puritans targeted the institution of the episcopate, James I had this to say: "no bishops, no king, no nobility."

This is in fact what almost happened under the following reign and under Cromwell.

As the seventeenth century began, this properly theological dispute took on new importance. It no longer concerned the Catholics; their fate had long been settled. They are limited to the little isolated camp of "recusants" who clustered around a few great families. But this dispute brings about a more and more defined breach between Anglicans and other Protestants. Anglicans become aware that they are not Calvinists.

England is in fact in constant communication with the two great laboratories of Protestant theology, Switzerland and especially Holland. The *Confessio Belgica*, just like the Heidelberg catechism, did not take a clear position on whether divine election was entirely arbitrary or whether it could depend on a person's faith, or even merely on divine foreknowledge of that faith. Pure Calvinism, in its exaltation of God's omnipotence, tended more and more toward God's arbitrary choice. The debate became focused on two champions: Arminius, a former believer in predestination who had turned toward liberalism, and his colleague Gomar of the University of Leyden, who situated election even before Adam's fall. The debate was infused with politics, because Arminians were favored by the States, the municipal governments of the merchant bourgeoisie, and the Gomarists by the Stadhouder Maurice of Nassau and the partisans of authoritarian centralization. Arminius's theses were condemned by the Canons of Dort in 1618–1619. These canons were severe.

In Canon X we read that election "does not involve God having chosen certain qualities or human actions among all those possible as a condition of salvation, but rather involves adopting certain particular persons from among the common mass of sinners as God's own possession. [...] (XI) the election made by him can neither be suspended nor altered, revoked, or annulled; neither can God's chosen ones be cast off, nor their number reduced." Moreover, (XII) "assurance of their eternal and unchangeable election to salvation is given to the chosen in due time." Do the damned also know it? This is less clear. In any case, they must not be discouraged, but "continue diligently" (XVI) "with reverent adoration" of God's Justice." (XVIII).

Many Protestants balk at such a hard doctrine. The Anglicans, for their part, protest. Their theologians, led by Andrews, are resolutely Arminian and very little inclined to the doctrine of predestination. Laud steered between Calvinism and Catholicism. In the good tradition of Anglicanism, he was more latitudinarian concerning doctrine and located the principle of unity and of spiritual life of the church in the magnificence of its liturgy. He re-institutes stained glass with figures and east-facing altars. When he becomes the Archbishop of Canterbury, Catholics take hope; there was some question of conferring upon him the Cardinal's crimson. However, he said, "somewhat dwelt within me that would not suffer that till Rome were other than it is." This "somewhat," an instinctive and visceral antipapism, grounded at bottom in national feeling, always constitutes the almost invisible but impenetrable boundary between Roman Catholicism and Anglican "Anglo-Catholicism," the Anglicanism that is most suffused with Catholic faith and most ostentatious in its liturgy.

Anglican religious liberalism drew from a still vital Erastian tradition. It led to rationalism; it did not lead to freedom of conscience. It was only the sectarians and the "Independents" who demanded freedom for its own sake and not simply, like the Erastian party, for political reasons.

Nevertheless, the revolution had begun. It started in Scotland, as an uprising against the tyranny of the Anglican episcopate. The Puritan movement had not forgiven Charles I for his marriage to Henriette of France, an ardent Catholic. He tried to resist the uprising, cutting the ears off a few Presbyterians, but was forced to convoke Parliament in 1640, something he had not done since 1629. Presbyterians and "Independents" made up a majority in this Parliament, in which a representative from Cambridge, Oliver Cromwell, distinguished himself. Laud and Strafford, abandoned by the King, were executed. Still civil war broke out. A "covenant" was signed between the anti-Episcopalians of Scotland and England. In 1644, Cromwell, a passionate Protestant at the head of the

New Model Army, charging with the cry "the Lord of Hosts," won two brilliant victories. The King was taken prisoner after a long search throughout the kingdom and executed the following year (1647).

Now the question was how the Puritan movement was going to succeed in changing England's religion. The Presbyterian model was available: it was a stable one, already long established in Scotland. Parliament set up an ecclesiastical committee, the Westminster Assembly, for the purpose of giving the whole kingdom a new ecclesiastical constitution.

The Westminster Confession

The main document to come out of this gathering, the Westminster Confession, was adopted first by the Scots and then by the English in Parliament in 1648. It is a remarkable text for the extreme clarity of its writing and for the influence it exercised over all reformed churches, particularly in the American colonies. Since it offers a synthesis of the state of Calvinism in the middle of the seventeenth century, it is worth providing some characteristic excerpts.

Of the Holy Scripture: "The authority of the Holy Scripture, for which it ought to be believed, and obeyed, depends not upon the testimony of any man, or Church; but wholly upon God (who is truth itself) the author thereof ...

"The whole counsel of God concerning all things necessary for His own glory, man's salvation, faith and life, is either expressly set down in Scripture, or by good and necessary consequence may be deduced from Scripture... Nevertheless, we acknowledge the inward illumination of the Spirit of God to be necessary for the saving understanding of such things as are revealed in the Word.

"Of God's Eternal Decree: "By the decree of God, for the manifestation of His glory, some men and angels are predestinated unto everlasting life; and others foreordained to everlasting death. ... their number so certain and definite, that it cannot be either increased or diminished.

"[T]hey who are elected, being fallen in Adam, are redeemed

by Christ, are effectually called unto faith in Christ by His Spirit working in due season, are justified, adopted, sanctified, and kept by His power, through faith, unto salvation.

"The rest of mankind God was pleased, according to the unsearchable counsel of His own will, whereby He extends or withholds mercy, as He pleases, for the glory of His sovereign power over His creatures, to pass by; and to ordain them to dishonor and wrath for their sin, to the praise of His glorious justice."

Of Providence: "Although, in relation to the foreknowledge and decree of God, the first Cause, all things come to pass immutably, and infallibly; yet, by the same providence, He orders them to fall out, according to the nature of second causes, either necessarily, freely, or contingently."

God delivers his children to numerous temptations "to chastise them for their former sins, or to discover unto them the hidden strength of corruption and deceitfulness of their hearts, that they may be humbled..." As for the wicked and impious, "He not only withholds His grace whereby they might have been enlightened in their understandings, and wrought upon in their hearts; but sometimes also withdraws the gifts which they had, and exposes them to such objects as their corruption makes occasion of sin..."

Of Sin: The corruption of nature, which makes us incapable of any good work, remains even among the regenerate, and "both itself, and all the motions thereof, are truly and properly sin." "Every sin, both original and actual, being a transgression of the righteous law of God, and contrary thereunto, does in its own nature, bring guilt upon the sinner, whereby he is bound over to the wrath of God, and curse of the law, and so made subject to death." By his fall into the state of sin, man is deprived of his free will and he has "wholly lost all ability of will to any spiritual good accompanying salvation."

Of Justification: "God did, from all eternity, decree to justify all the elect, and Christ did, in the fullness of time, die for their sins, and rise again for their justification: nevertheless, they are not justified, until the Holy Spirit does, in due time, actually apply Christ unto them." The justified can sin, but cannot fall from their state of justification. By grace, and by the warfare of the Spirit against the Flesh, "the saints grow in grace, perfecting holiness in the fear of God."

Of Assurance of Salvation: "such as truly believe in the Lord Jesus, and love Him in sincerity, endeavoring to walk in all good conscience before Him, may, in this life, be certainly assured that they are in the state of grace... This certainty is not a bare conjectural and probable persuasion grounded upon a fallible hope; but an infallible assurance..."

Political and Social Positions:

Of Christian Liberty, and Liberty of Conscience: "God alone is Lord of the conscience, and has left it free from the doctrines and commandments of men..." Nevertheless—and this practically annuls the preceding: "They who, upon pretence of Christian liberty, do practice any sin, or cherish any lust, do thereby destroy the end of Christian liberty, which is, that being delivered out of the hands of our enemies, we might serve the Lord without fear... they who, upon pretence of Christian liberty, shall oppose any lawful power, or the lawful exercise of it, whether it be civil or ecclesiastical, resist the ordinance of God." They expose themselves to legitimate punishment at the hands of Church as well as State authorities.

Of Religious Worship, and the Sabbath Day: "This Sabbath is to be kept holy unto the Lord when men, after a due preparing of their hearts, and ordering of their common affairs beforehand, do not only observe an holy rest all the day from their own works, words, and thoughts about their worldly employments and recreations, but also are taken up the whole time in the public and private exercises of His worship, and in the duties of necessity and mercy."

Of the Civil Magistrate: God "ordained civil magistrates ... and ... has armed them with the power of the sword, for the defense and encouragement of them that are good, and for the punishment of evil doers. It is lawful for Christians to accept and execute the office of a magistrate, when called thereunto... they may lawfully... wage war...The civil magistrate has authority, and it is his duty, to take order that unity and peace be preserved in the Church, that the truth of God be kept pure and entire, that all blasphemies and heresies be suppressed, all corruptions and abuses in worship and discipline prevented or reformed, and all the ordinances of God duly settled, administrated, and observed. ...It is the duty of people to pray for magistrates, to honor their persons, to pay them tribute or other dues, to obey their lawful commands, and to be subject to their authority, for conscience' sake ..."

In this political part of the Westminster Confession, we see the polemical point against the radical reformers, who will eventually carry the day. The Confession sets limits to liberty of conscience and defines the rights of the state in spiritual matters. On points of doctrine, the sacraments, divorce, the church, the holy supper, the permissibility of divorce in the case of adultery, the anti-Christian character of the Pope of Rome, and the negation of purgatory, it is hardly distinguishable from classic Calvinism or from the Book of Common Prayer of Edward VI. In addition it gives another turn of the screw to the English Sunday.

Revolutionary Decomposition

The Puritan movement was a product of the decomposition of the English Episcopalian system. The triumph of the Presbyterians, which was supposed to bring English reform to completion and produce a definitive stability, lasted only an instant. Disintegration affected Presbyterianism itself. Parliament had decided, at the close of the Westminster assembly, that Presbyterianism would be the system for all of England (October 1647). But loyalty to the king and to bishops still existed in many parts of society and the Westminster assembly, before convening, had promised to respect such loyalty. Moreover, the revolution continued. That is, Parliament itself depended more and more on the army, which was heavily influenced by the radical and sectarian "Independents." In order to depict the climate that reigned in this army, consider this report from one who was present at its councils: "we consecrated a day to prayer, a second again to prayer and to seeking God in the Scripture. Cromwell then exhorted us to a severe examination of our actions in order to find the cause of divine chastisement. We confessed our sins to one another, and our sobs made it barely possible to speak. Finally the Lord directed our efforts." In effect, in this council the decision was taken to take the King prisoner and to punish him for "the blood that he has spilled and the much damage that he has done to the Lord's cause and to that of this poor nation." (Léonard)

It is strange to behold the proliferation of hundreds of independent congregations that are born beginning in the 1640s. These are groups of the elect, certain of their salvation, who derive from this certainty a total liberty in relation to all clergy, and sometimes from all masters. The testimony of the Holy Spirit, one of the pillars of Calvinist doctrine, is now understood as a "light within," which can sometimes mean a mystical illumination reserved to the "spiritual" alone, and sometimes the simple dictates of reason. These are the People of God, through a personal covenant. They obey His law and await His kingdom, with a confidence that contrasts with Calvinist pessimism. Sin has no more power over them, and, among the antinomians, sin does not even have any importance—not even sins of the flesh among the Ranters. These groups are born and die rapidly. At the base of each one finds a cell of militants, and at the summit a council of equals of a dozen members. They gather contributions and print pamphlets and petitions.

Some of the sects have a political and social orientation. The sect of the Levelers is the most important among these; for a moment the authority of its leader, Lilburne, rivals that of Cromwell. It demands a reform of voting rights and total freedom of conscience, which means the abandonment of a national church to the benefit of churches independent of one another. A pamphlet of 1647 demands the abolition of the tithe and introduces the principle that the source and foundation of power is in popular consent. In a debate held in the church of the village of Putney, a suburb of London, where Cromwell had agreed to participate, the Levelers go so far as to propose, in the name of the birthright of every free Englishman, a moderate form of universal suffrage. Domestic servants and paid workers would be excluded.

After the execution of the king, the Rump Parliament decides the abolition of the monarchy and of the House of Lords, and confides the government to what remains of the Commons and to a council of state, the two organs now dominated by Cromwell. This was the complete defeat of the hopes of Lilburne and of the Levelers. Power was falling into the hands of an oligarchy beyond all control. The Army was restless and Cromwell cracked down: Lilburne was on his way to the Tower. The group called Diggers tried to take the place of the Levelers and went further in its social program. All man's misfortunes come from private property. "This private property of mine and thine is the cause of human misfortune. First it leads men to steal. Then it is the source of laws that punish thieves with hanging" (Himy). The Diggers, like social utopians who preceded and followed them, extolled a simple rural life, autarkic and communitarian. But they also reaffirmed that man is born free by virtue of his birthright, a concept that anticipates the idea of human rights.

Other sects define themselves by their theological orientation. As theological disputation is systematically discouraged in the established church, it becomes all the more ardent on the dissident margins. A whole range of theological positions emerges in this amazing decade. Along with the Presbyterians and the Baptists, there are the Antinomians, the Seekers (Quietists), the Ranters, the Perfectionists (hyper Pelagians), and the Mortalists, who deny the immortality of the soul. The old Gnosticism clothes itself in the teachings of the Rosicrucians, of the Familist disciples of Boehme, and soon of Free Masonry.

One of the most interesting sects embellishes on theology and politics: the Fifth Monarchy. It arises from among the ranks of the "independents," and more precisely from the alliance between the "independents" and the Army. No sooner had the king been executed—January 30, 1649—than a petition demanded that the Kingdom of Christ be immediately established, with the government of the Saints. The hope was that England would constitute a new Zion, that the Bible would be the law of a new state, and that the government of Saints would be "the administration of the gospel."

This is an example of the apocalyptic millenarianism that expands like a bubble during this short period of the English revolution. The church, the new elect, is decimated by a bloody persecution instigated by Satan. Finally, after the exhaustion of scourges and the opening of the Seven Seals, the beast is destroyed and Christ comes to reign for a thousand years. These themes of the Apocalypse, together with those of Daniel and of the Five Kingdoms, are adapted to England. John Fox applies to England, the new elect people who fight the Pope, the figure of the Christ and the antichrist. The end of the world is imminent, and the present struggle of the Puritans and of the revolution is its sign. The overthrow of the Pope-antichrist announces the millennium. Christ and his saints shall reign upon the earth.

This scheme, which was very widespread, is reinforced by a mystical numerology, which interprets the dates of contemporary events as prophetic signs. 1666 is the year of the beast. Napier, the inventor of logarithms, announces the fall of the Roman church in 1639 and the end of the world in 1688. Newton passed an infinite amount of time on the same kind of speculations.

Even though the humble and the poor have a particular role to play in the cosmic battle, the people must not be confused with the multitude, nor with the people in the sense this term takes under the French revolution. The multitude lends its support to those who oppose the antichrist. The people of God are only the people of the saints, in practice the little number of those who are faithful and well-instructed in Scripture, whose responsibility it is to establish the government of Zion. Christ has given his power to the church, but this is not an Episcopalian hierarchy, nor a national Presbyterian Church, but a group of Saints assembled in a congregation.

It is time for us to leave England and follow those who gathered in its ports and equipped ships to cross the Atlantic. They were leaving behind them an England that had passed the highest point of the revolution. The political revolution was only achieved later, and the religious revolution was only suspended by the Restoration. The Anglican Church was re-established as supreme, but it had gone through a long dry period. It is divided in into a "Laudian," traditionalist part, and a rationalist part that is persuaded that reason is the sovereign arbiter of both natural and revealed religion. This is the thinking of the Cambridge Platonists. The tendency is toward deism, and also toward a certain toleration. This toleration might, at the limit, be extended to include Catholics; the violent refusal of this policy was one of the causes of the fall of the Stuarts and of the final resolution of the political revolution. Still the Anglican Church retained enough vitality to give rise from within itself to the surprising rebirth associated with the great name of Wesley.

Might we risk a concluding observation? The French Revolution gave rise to two forces that transformed the modern world, nationalism of the Jacobin type and socialism. But the English Revolution, having taken place in a pre-ideological age, was the laboratory that produced, apart from the representative and parliamentary system that the French Revolution and its repercussions spread to the European continent, most of the religious forces (transformed to be sure by the local climate of America) that now, since the end of the twentieth century, are making themselves felt in the rest of the world.

Lutheran and Calvinist ideas had entered precociously into England. They mixed with other traditions and branched out in various directions. One of these is the strict Calvinism of the Presbyterians. There also arose esoteric speculations, which are the origin in particular of Freemasonry, at least in the line of the Rosicrucianism of the semi-English court of Heidelberg. Baptist currents also took root, and with them Congregationalism. And an autochthonous millenarianism inspired the most militant branch of the English revolution and engendered a host of sects. Some of these are ephemeral, others long-lasting, such as the Quakers, who are only one branch of an evangelical movement still living today.

If not for the development of the United States, this laboratory might have vegetated and perhaps disappeared little by little. The established religion benefited from state support, and from laws that guaranteed it the monopoly of high offices, the direction and the exclusive recruitment of the universities, the education and the maintenance of a clergy that covered the whole of England down to its smallest villages. Two points of resistance remained: Presbyterianism, concentrated in the quasi-nation of Scotland, and a residual Catholicism. All other religious creations were thus condemned to live on the margins, in the interstices left by the three solidly organized religious blocs.

In the great spaces of America, even before independence, all these bodies, legal or dissident, were put on an equal footing and in competition. They prospered unequally. But those that had the most success now give Protestantism its new face. Lutheranism is limited to the Germanic part of Europe—except when it accompanies German and Scandinavian immigrants to the New World. Calvinism is still alive in Europe, but as a minority, even in Geneva. America sets the tone, and England enters little by little into its orbit. The new forms of the Reformation, what now is called evangelical Protestantism, benefit from the vitality, the prestige, and the power of the United States, which has become the sun from which they radiate out to the whole world.

IV.
AMERICA

My subject is American Protestantism. One might say that I am late coming to it. In fact I have never left it.

America is complicated, because all of Europe in its diversity was transported there. Though rebellious, she is the direct heir of England, whose religious history is not simple. She is also related in various degrees to the other nations with whom England was involved, and which arrived successively on her coasts. Each one brought its baggage.

It has been necessary to take the time to research the origin and the importance of each of these factors.

Like the customs official at Ellis Island, America has had to be selective. He accepted some contributions entirely and others only partially. Others he had to pass over, for good or for ill. Those who arrive do not always know what they are bringing with them, or they do not remember. This is why I am so late in coming to the heart of my subject: in fact I have almost covered it. There remains little more than the reporting of events. The great theological choices, which will give meaning to these events, have already been taken.

American Religious Exceptionalism

When a European, let's say a Frenchman, first visits an American city, he is struck by the number of churches. Many are needed in fact because the Christian religion is divided into a multitude of confessions and, in order to meet religious needs, there must be local places of worship for Calvinists, Lutherans, Catholics,

Episcopalians, etc. This multiplication is further accentuated by the Congregationalist spirit. Each group makes up an autonomous whole, which governs itself within a given "denomination." This is why you will see in the same city, not far from each other, in a pretty Georgian or neo-Palladian style, little red and white churches of brick or painted wood, which bear the name of First, Second, or Third Baptist Church, Church of Christ, Methodist, Disciples of Christ, etc. The Frenchman who enters these places of worship on a Sunday will find it full of people. Accustomed to Sunday masses in France, to their scattered attendance of old ladies, he is surprised by the diversity of ages of both sexes and by the social level that corresponds to the demography of the area.

According to a poll conducted in 2001, only 14% of Americans claim no religious attachment or confession. In 1990 the number was only 8%. Free thought is thus progressing rapidly. 20% of Americans attend a religious service at least once a week. (This actual practice is less than the declared practice of 40%.) But this is still very far from the French figures, where weekly Sunday worship is less than 5% (Lacorne).

This persistence of religious attachment is all the more surprising since the Founding Fathers were not particularly pious. Franklin and Jefferson were more deist than Christian, and Adams went over to Unitarianism, a rationalist version of the original Calvinism. The Philadelphia convention rejected Franklin's proposal that daily sessions be opened with prayer. Adams also wished that the United States declare itself a Christian nation. Madison, a liberal Christian, rejected this point of view. In defending total religious liberty, he took up the argument that Voltaire had placed at the end of his *English Letters*: if there is only one religion, it oppresses; if there are two, they are at each other's throats; if there are 100, they are forced to tolerate each other. When "denominations" are scattered and as numerous as possible, they lose the principal means of their malignant will, the power of the state (Federalist 51). The argument is excellent from the point of view of civil peace, but it represents a bracketing of the truth. This is an English heritage. The Anglican compromise had avoided over-emphasis on doctrine; piety could do without it. Distrust of overly precise and elaborate definitions of doctrine remains a constant of American religion.

The most sacred text, which has by far the most authority and stability on which everything rests, is the text of the Constitution approved in 1797. It contains no reference to God. It prohibits all religious tests for public employment. The only authority is the people: "We the people of the United States …" Some have spoken of a godless Constitution. The First Amendment stipulates: "Congress shall make no law respecting an establishment of religion, or prohibiting the free exercise thereof …"

Thus, at the end of the eighteenth century, one might have predicted that religion would follow the course of Anglicanism in England, of which Joseph de Maistre said that it only ceased to persecute in ceasing to be Christian; or of Catholicism in France, which withered along with the progress of the Enlightenment. Yet, despite this Whig, deist, or atheist point of departure, American religion followed a radically different course.

Discord between a fervent and widespread Christianity and legal secularism remains unresolved, however. The partisans of a "Christian nation" still strive to maintain prayer in schools, Sabbath observance, the display of the Ten Commandments in courthouses, etc. The theory of evolution is the object of public criticism that one might say is semi-doctrinal insofar as this theory is opposed to biblical literalism. Prohibition and laws regulating secular morality, extending even to the bedroom of married persons, can follow from the commitment to a "Christian nation." The secular party, the result of a surprising political alliance in the name of freedom between deist rationalists of Jefferson's type and evangelical minorities, dissident or Baptists, who reject an established Church, has stood firm. In all later struggles it has regularly prevailed.

The Constitution was still new when, in 1801, a great evangelical gathering was held in Cane Ridge, Kentucky, which is considered to be the starting point of the Second Great Awakening (after that of 1730–1760). This showed the ongoing tension between the secular (but not antireligious) party, and that of "the Christian nation" as a public confession.

This phenomenon has not escaped the attention of European sociologists (Boudon).

Adam Smith had already noticed that irreligion was growing in England, but not in the United States. Observing the multiplicity of American sects, he argued that the competitive American system allowed each believer to find the church that suited him. In England, one who wishes to leave the Anglican Church, which benefits from a legal monopoly, must take a step down into the world of "dissent", which renders the believer vulnerable to various forms of harassment, to marginalization, or at worst to persecution. In America, one has only to change churches, and since one can find another at the next street corner, one is less tempted by irreligion.

Tocqueville wrote: "in America, religion has so to speak set its own limits; the religious order there has remained entirely distinct from the political order, so that they were able to change ancient laws easily without shaking ancient beliefs." In the old France, religion was intimately bound up with the monarchical system, and it was impossible to overturn the monarchy without uprooting the church. The complete separation between the state and the churches thus explains their peaceful relations. But Tocqueville does not explain the persistence of religious fervor.

Tocqueville observes that, despite the fragmentation of denominations, they all see themselves as belonging to the same Protestant family: "in the United States there is an infinite variety of Christian sects, but Christianity itself is an established and irresistible fact." The basis of this nebulous community of belief is more moral than dogmatic. Belief detaches itself from doctrine and doctrine from truth: it is an opinion and, as one says, a "persuasion." In a Catholic country, church membership rests upon adherence to a set of truths laid out in credos, in the proclamations of councils, and in authoritative decrees, and this adherence is publicly confessed and monitored. A heretic is expelled from the communion of the faithful, and, under the *Ancien Régime*, from the civil community. In the new order, doctrinal discipline conflicts more and more with scientific progress, and it is both less feared and more detested.

Moreover, as the state takes over education and welfare, the church is little by little deprived of its functions. Stripped of its goods and purposes, cut off from the movement of thought, nothing remains of the Catholic Church in France but nostalgia, charitable and missionary work, and sometimes holiness.

In America, on the contrary, the churches are useful and are the required path to the good conduct of life, both material and moral. Democratic individualism progresses apace in religion as in politics. Religion is "immanentized" (Boudon). The question of truth no longer arises, since opinions are infinitely variable, without giving rise to religious skepticism. All persuasions are respectable, because in a democracy they are all on an equal footing. The spirit of religion loses its sacredness within each denomination, but it recovers it insofar as it envelops religion as a whole and is bound up with the sacredness of the democratic constitution and with that of the nation as a whole, that of the American people, a city upon a hill. Each denomination is devalued, but religion in general holds sway all the more. It matters little which religion, for the American chooses it freely, but it is necessary that he have one.

Max Weber observes that in fact all the denominations are not equal. There are some that are more equal than others, and these are the oldest. He cites the Lutherans who arrived from Germany in the first third of the nineteenth century, who were solidly established and achieved a high level of social respectability. But still more status may be gained by moving to a still older layer. "The sects are providers of symbols of social status." Today, for one of already high status, to convert to the Episcopalian religion is a further step up. Since Episcopalianism is quite liberal in matters of faith, and since it carries a fashionable odor of old England, and often boasts the biggest and most beautiful churches, it is understandable that it can crown a particularly successful career.

In this way sociological analysis gives a satisfactory account of the survival of Christianity in the United States, just as it accounts for its rapid decline in Western Europe, Protestant as well as Catholic. But sociology cannot search the hearts where faith resides.

The Puritan Matrix

We must now go back a bit.

In the very violent religious struggles that agitated England between the National-Catholicism of Henry VIII and the late-arriving stabilization brought about by the Elizabethan compromise, a number of projects arose for the establishment of places of "refuge" for dissidents on the American coast. It was the Puritan refuge that was most successful and that left its imprint on religious America.

Elizabeth's compromise was not something concluded between Catholics and Protestants. The excommunication of the Queen in 1570 (the bull *Regnans in excelsis*) released subjects from their allegiance, and thus turned Catholics into traitors and potential terrorists. The defeat of the Armada, dispersed by a "Protestant wind," showed which side God was on (1588). The Gunpowder Plot was a patent act of terrorism (1605). Catholics were no longer interlocutors for any kind of compromise. They had put themselves outside of the English nation and would only return officially in 1829.

The national religion was equipped with founding texts. In 1559 Parliament had voted the Supremacy and Uniformity Acts, by which the Queen became the supreme "governor" of the Church of England. The *Book of Common Prayer* was accompanied by a list of Thirty-Nine Articles that in principle defined the credo of the English. It is very skillfully drafted and can be read in many ways. It can be understood in a way very close to Catholic orthodoxy, as was the hope of Newman and his friends in the Oxford Movement around 1820. According to another interpretation, it maintains the three founding principles of the Reformation (*sola gratia, sola fide, sola scriptura*), predestination, and the elimination of all sacraments but baptism and the Lord's Supper.

This compromise, the conditions of which were thus settled by texts, aimed at reconciliation among Protestants alone. It did not succeed.

A significant Protestant party nevertheless believed that the national church was polluted by residues that were pagan, anti-Christian, and, when all is said and done, Catholic. The test was "scriptural traceability" (Henneton). "If one could find a justification for such and such a point of organization or ritual, then it was acceptable." Otherwise it was human invention and corruption. Did the Bible justify the wearing of the surplice, the sign of the cross at the moment of baptism, or genuflection during the sacrament of the Last Supper? The English had got rid of the Pope; did they have to keep the bishops?

Puritanism is less a doctrine than a movement. It exists in different degrees of radicalism. The Presbyterians, following the example of the continental Calvinist churches, advocated a pyramidal structure, capped by a national synod, with subordinate regional synods. Congregationalists held that each community was independent and not accountable to anyone. Members elected pastors and elders.

The Puritans wanted only to reform the Church of England "from the inside." But when a group, led by Pastor Browne, realized that this was not possible, they *separated*. Persecuted, they went into exile, first in the Netherlands, and then, from there, to the American colonies. In 1620, the 200 passengers of the Mayflower landed at Plymouth; the following year, in order to thank God for having saved them from famine during their first winter, normally the deadliest, they celebrated the first Thanksgiving with a feast.

The Faith of the Puritans

At the beginning of his history, *Of Plymouth Plantation*, Gov. Bradford described Satan as "loath that his kingdom should go down, the truth prevail, and the churches of God revert to their ancient purity [...] according to the simplicity of the gospel, without a mixture of men's inventions." Such in effect was the program of the Pilgrims.

They were Protestant. They professed justification by faith, in the sense that each individual person can accept God's offer of salvation and accept to be its beneficiary. The person becomes confidently aware that this offer is addressed to him personally, and he believes in it. Faith is the guarantee of salvation. He refuses to grant the slightest value to the virtue of a sacerdotal act or a ritual external to religious experience itself. The question of knowing whether he is saved or not is posed only between God and himself. The Bible and the meditation of the Bible are the principal means of relation to God; it is subject only to personal judgment. The authority of the document, the word of God freely interpreted, is set in opposition to any institution that would wish to mediate.

They were Calvinists. The Synod of Dort (1618) had laid down five "points of doctrine" that defined a good theology. It defined predestination in terms that excluded all human participation in the work of salvation. It rejected any understanding of election having another cause than God's good pleasure alone. It did not accept the idea that the efficacy of divine grace depended on an individual's negative or affirmative response, nor the idea that the grace given to the elect could be lost.

This synod condemned Arminianism, since it makes God's election depend on man's will, extenuates and abolishes the grace of God, lifts up man and the strength of his free will in order to throw him down to perdition, brings back Pelagianism, disguises Papism, and overturns all certainty of salvation. Arminius was a pastor, and professor at the University of Leiden. He questioned double predestination (both to salvation and to damnation), and he believed that man could accept the grace offered to all by a free act of his will, and therefore minimized the extent of original sin and the radical corruption of our nature that was its consequence. His adversary and colleague at the same university, Gomar, affirmed that predestination had been decreed by God even before he created humanity and permitted the fall; this was called supralapsarian predestination.

The victory of Gomar and of strict Calvinism at the Synod of Dort was a pyrrhic victory. The Arminian teaching had in fact already won the contest in the Church of England, where it was combined with the Erasmian trend that had been strong since the beginning of the Renaissance. It was also shared by the modern, commercial and secular part of Dutch society, which was spontaneously "latitudinarian." It might be argued that the whole history of Protestantism in the United States is that of a gradual dilution of Gomar's teaching and a victory of the Arminian theses, even if few remember these professors whose quarrel tore up the Netherlands.

The first breach was brought about by "Covenant Theology." Its most distinguished representative, John Cotton, tried to preserve Calvinism and its "five points of doctrine," at least formally, but he defended "the value of reason, the regularity of second causes in nature, the harmony between knowledge and faith, the convergence in God between goodness and will, the intimate connection between grace and the motives that bring it about, and (especially) the necessity of moral responsibility and of action" (Perry). One must act as if salvation depended upon oneself, but at the same time attribute spiritual progress to God. The effort of reason and the voice of moral conscience provide motives that prepare supernatural faith and accord with it. Cotton would have trembled if one had pointed out to him that St. Ignatius of Loyola had recommended that we "act as if everything depended upon oneself and pray as if everything depended upon God." The covenant, or the compact of grace, is a contract between God and man. God has committed himself by defining the condition of salvation (faith). He gave the elect the power to respond to this commitment. Justified by grace, the elect enjoy the dignity of holding their heads high and claiming their rights in the very presence of God, who granted them. The Puritans are enterprising, self-confident, and, observing the continual progress of their undertakings, believe that, by virtue of the covenant, heaven helps those who help themselves.

The great thinker of the first half of the eighteenth century is Jonathan Edwards (1703–1752), educated at Yale, who died just after being named president of the college that will later be known as Princeton University. His strength and weakness consisted in joining pure Calvinism with philosophy, which introduced a certain tension in his thought (Baritz).

He was one of the greatest preachers of the Awakening. Here is the tone of one of his sermons:

O sinner! Consider the fearful danger you are in: it is a great furnace of wrath, a wide and bottomless pit, full of the fire of wrath, that you are held over in the hand of that God, whose wrath is provoked and incensed as much against you, as against many of the damned in hell. ...If you cry to God to pity you, he will be so far from pitying you in your doleful case, or showing you the least regard or favour, that instead of that, he will only tread you under foot. And though he will know that you cannot bear the weight of omnipotence treading upon you, yet he will not regard that, but he will crush you under his feet without mercy; he will crush out your blood, and make it fly, and it shall be sprinkled on his garments, so as to stain all his raiment.

This God, who seems like a butcher, is less lovable than the way he is represented today.

Jonathan Edwards was appalled by Arminianism and was considered a strict Calvinist. If everything having to do with salvation is up to God, this can result in fatalism, and at the limit in antinomianism, examples of which were known to Luther's Germany. If one increases the human contribution, one risks sliding toward Pelagius, or worse, toward Papism. For Calvin, the moment of human salvation coincides with God's act of choosing it. Grace is irresistible. According to the covenant, man can only be saved after having shown that he deserves salvation. Against this theology, the laxity of which horrified him, Edwards affirmed that only the converted may be invited to the holy supper and that only their children can be candidates for baptism.

Edwards affirmed, according to the experience of the awakening, that the affections are an essential part of religious life, and that their spiritual authenticity must be examined according to rigorous criteria. He discovers twelve of these. Through the inclusion of these emotional elements, Edwards comes close, unknowingly and despite himself, to the Methodists and Baptists, who were arriving by the boat-full in the colony.

What was problematic in his doctrine was that he appealed to other sources than the Bible, and that, in order to defend the exclusive role of God, he sought out arguments in the philosophy of the Cambridge Platonists and especially in Locke, of whom he was one of the first readers in America. Rather than contenting himself with the simple face-to-face of the Christian with God, accessible only by his Word, he constructs a rational system that encompasses this face-to-face in a philosophy of the whole, by which he explains both necessity and freedom. He *proves* Calvinism. The human will is governed by causes, which, in turn, express God's nature. There exists a general harmony, which the Christian divines by a special sense. He chooses what he believes to be good. The human will is governed by motives which, if they are right, express the nature of God. The creation manifests the love that God bears to himself, and his nature is nothing other than the harmony between beauty and love. "Thus also, when he decrees diligence and industry, he decrees riches and prosperity; when he decrees prudence, he often decrees success; when he decrees striving, then he often decrees the obtaining the kingdom of heaven." There is a harmonious relationship among all these gifts. God decrees them all together as the partial elements of his overall plan. He may allow evil in order to give more scope to holiness. One must love God such as he is. In this way Edwards believes he reconciles, by an intuition of the glory of God, the omnipotence of grace with the value of human efforts, predestination and freedom.

The Great Awakening

Awakenings are recurrent phenomena in American religious life. An English Anglican sent to observe in 1742, right in the middle of the Great Awakening (1730–1760), came back stunned. "It is impossible to relate the convulsions into which the whole country is thrown by a set of enthusiasts that stroll about haranguing the admiring vulgar ... Men, women, children, servants and negroes now become (as they phrased it) exhorters." According to Henneton, the theological basis of the first Great Awakening was a combination of New England Puritanism, German pietism, and rationalism inspired by Locke. But the innovation lies in the new importance attributed to the experience of conversion. It is a new birth in Christ; it is an instantaneous transformation of the soul, henceforth redeemed and inflamed by the promise of eternal salvation.

Whitefield was the most famous of the preachers. He hypnotized his listeners. He is supposed to have preached 18,000 sermons before immense crowds. He touched hearts, and he collected money. His type is still alive; Billy Graham still illustrates this tradition. Graham is the most famous of the "entrepreneurs of salvation" who are a permanent figure of religious life, as is shown today by the "televangelists" and the gigantic mega-churches.

Whitefield and the others practiced a ministry of fear. They evoked again and again the specter of damnation, the risk of dying without having sincerely converted. Songs and hymns reinforced emotion, and sharpened spiritual insecurity. The faithful rolled on the ground, burst out in tears, and fainted. Edwards's uncle, in despair over the state of his soul, fell ill and killed himself. In his famous sermon, "sinners in the hands of an angry God," Edwards conjured up the burning furnace, raging waters, a spider hanging by a thread over the fire, a nice comparison with the sinful man hanging over the flames of hell. Some enthusiasts went further still. One almost drowned because he had been inspired, like Moses, to strike a large river with his rod. It is in these years that we see the appearance of the itinerant preacher, who belongs to no regular confession, following his own initiative and moved by the inner light. He is in competition with regularly ordained pastors. He sets out for the West all alone, risking confrontations with Indians and the loss of his scalp.

In the end the Great Awakening subsided. Pastors such as Davenport, Chauncey, and Tennant denounced the whole business as "enthusiasm," a pejorative term in the English enlightenment. They also feared excesses leading to Baptism, which had been present in the colonies from the founding years. They feared the "separatism" of these churches, of which one could not become a member without a voluntary and conscious process, or without a baptism administered at the age of adult.

Awakenings return periodically. There is another in 1801 and again the Second Great Awakening of 1857. One can no doubt consider the wave of piety that swept over America in Eisenhower's day, which put "in God we trust" on the dollar bill and added "under God" to the Pledge of Allegiance, as another awakening. One can even see the great movement of civil rights from this perspective, and, in another spirit, the movement of the Moral Majority, founded in 1979 by Jerry Falwell, which contributed to the election of President Reagan. In these later waves the mark of Puritanism is still visible, though much effaced.

Puritan Politics

The Puritans' goal was to build pure communities on the far shore of the Atlantic. They respected the traceability test and resolved to draw rules of conduct from the Bible, if possible only from the Bible. An English child, having opened the Bible at random in order to find an oracular sign, fell upon the following verse: "Wherefore come out from among them, and be ye separate, saith the Lord, and touch not the unclean thing; and I will receive you, and will be a Father unto you, and ye shall be my sons and daughters, saith the Lord Almighty." With the blessings of his parents he boarded the first available ship. Names were taken from the holy text: Sarah, Samuel, Josiah, and even Kill Sin and Fly Fornication. Beyond the permanent consultation of Scripture, the Puritan's duty was to listen to the sermon, which gave the pastor a central place in the community.

Still, one cannot speak of a full theocracy. There are no ecclesiastical courts, and pastors are forbidden from occupying civil offices. Puritan establishments follow the example of Calvin: the magistrate consults the pastor and the elders, but he is not required to follow their counsel. The civil (Aaron) and religious (Moses) spheres are distinct. The pastor admonishes the sinner; the magistrate punishes him. Both share the same faith. What is called

Puritan theocratic totalitarianism in the end had very few victims. The Salem witch trials ended in 19 executions. Catholic and Protestant Europe well surpassed this.

The church is a voluntary community and is not universal. It is a kind of club. It is not an English parish that includes everyone in a locality. It excludes the sinful multitude. The assembly gathers only the saints and administers baptism and the Holy Supper to them alone. Membership rules might vary according to the authority of certain pastors. For example, Cotton was a little more welcoming and Hooker more demanding. The aim was always to bring the Visible Church close to the Invisible Church of Heaven's elect. A member of this spiritual aristocracy is under obligation to attend the services and to listen to the Word. Within the same village he is distinguished from ordinary people who have no part in the holy community.

Moral Customs

Moral customs are rigorous in the extreme. A later essayist was able to write that "the Puritans were haunted by the fear that someone, somewhere might be happy" (Henneton). The virtues of abstinence and of continence might reach great heights, which in no way prevented the Puritans from engendering very large families. Edwards had nine children. American literature, from Hawthorne to Faulkner, is inexhaustible on the subject.

In the process of admission to a church, the candidate had to convince the saints that he had indeed received saving grace. We have documents in which the prospective member retraced the steps of his conversion and persuades the authorities of his predestination to salvation. These proofs have little to do with doctrine. The congregation was satisfied with a basic orthodoxy, generally taken from the Westminster Confession, supported by numerous scriptural citations. The civil magistrate was consulted on the good conduct of the applicant. Dogmatic expression was not in the Puritan spirit; respect for the Sabbath, violation of which was punished by whipping, counted more.

God alone can search hearts; what happens in the intimate relation of the soul with its Creator is not available to investigation. What can be observed is conduct. Blasphemy, lying, adultery, fornication and drunkenness: these are sins that can be seen and from which conversion delivers the believer. These are the tests that are used, not adherence to a systematic doctrine, which the Bible in principle renders superfluous. This is why the revolt against the Puritan spirit is not a revolt against beliefs, but against moral rules. Drinking, fornicating, smoking, cheating on one's wife (or today on one's partner)—such are the signs of rebellion against what is still called Puritanism, traces of which endure in all forms of American Christianity, even those that have decided to do without religion.

The Dilution of Puritanism

The pyramidal structure of Presbyterianism could not last long in New England. The separatist drift goes too well with the social structure of independent communities that are formed in the immense expanse of the colony. The Congregationalist tendency is irresistible. The church is simply the community of the faithful gathered in a given place. Each local church is autonomous and sovereign; each determines its confession of faith and its liturgy. The pastor's influence is based on his personality, but he cannot last long in contradiction with the community of the faithful. Not all the faithful share the taste for moral athleticism and for the repudiation of pleasure as exemplified by the saints. Congregationalism thus tends to push the community toward ordinary human ways. After the two first glorious decades of strict Puritanism, the churches had to accept the "halfway members" who could be accepted to baptism, but not to communion.

The main reason for the weakening of Puritanism was the formation of a religious market (Henneton). As long as they were able to maintain solidly controlled communities, the Puritans enjoyed a monopoly on the supply of religion. They could not prevent other propositions concerning salvation from appearing in their territory.

Other "denominations" offered their advantages, and, in this land of commerce and enterprise, religious pluralism took the form of a market in which Christians went, so to speak, from stall to stall and made their choices.

The Anglican Church occupied positions of dominance in the southern colonies, and important ones in the North, where they were in the minority and considered as dissidents. This "Episcopal" church had no bishops, because the English bishops found many reasons not to board ship. It rejected Puritan pessimism, held that the believer could in a certain measure work toward the salvation of his soul, and thus practiced a beneficent moralism, an obligation of good deeds. It tended toward an Arminianism colored by rationalism. Harvard University took liberalism to the point of Unitarianism, that is, to simplify, a religion within the limits of simple reason.

The market grew and diversified ceaselessly. Wave followed wave of immigration. The Wesleyans arrived from England. Wesley is an admirable Christian figure. This fellow of Lincoln College (Oxford) nourishes all the well-born Englishman's disgust with Papism. Still, to a Catholic eye he seems quite typical of the saints that the Council of Trent had put upon the altars. One is reminded of Saint Charles Borromeo or Saint Vincent de Paul. He had gathered in his college a circle of students devoted to a life of discipline and sanctification. They were called "Methodists." During a trip to Georgia, he encountered the Moravian Brothers, who initiated him in the mystical life. He flatly rejects Calvinist predestination. He affirms that the Christian, after his conversion, must give evidence of his regeneration by pious and well-ordered conduct, because he is not assured of eternal salvation, a point that brings him close to the Catholic position, though he doesn't know it. He preaches outside of the parishes, wherever people are to be found, in their homes or workplaces. He goes to the people. In America the Methodists separated from Anglicanism and created their own church, which then underwent many ruptures and reunifications. Wesley and his brother composed a beautiful and profound hymnody, which inspired the whole Protestant world. Negro spirituals often derive from these hymns. Methodism is a popular, charitable and benevolent form of Protestantism; the Salvation Army is an offshoot of it. It showed an early openness to the ecumenical movement, and, in the twentieth century, did not fear to enter into conversation with Catholicism. During the century between 1850 and 1950 it was the largest Protestant denomination. It organized camp meetings, those great pious gatherings that brought together pioneers, ranchers and cowboys from the Western prairies. These open-air meetings re-created the atmosphere of awakenings at the local level and for a short duration.

The Baptist wave reached its peak in the 1830s and 40s. Its doctrine is of a generally Calvinist inspiration. It emphasizes the sanctification of the Christian under the eye of a God who has no need of rituals in order to communicate with men. Each Baptist assembly is autonomous, and the pastor is elected by the members of the local church. Baptism thus benefits from the fundamentally congregationalist tendency that affects all the churches. It is normal then that we find Baptists among the fundamentalists (one of the founders of the Ku Klux Klan was Baptist) and that we also find social Christians, liberal theologians, and charismatics. The evangelical style is the dominant trait. The sign of membership is the convert's baptism by immersion, following a public testimony. In effect, there can be no conversion process if the one being baptized is not aware of what he is doing. Baptism is ordinarily administered at the age of adulthood. Purely intellectual adherence does not suffice. The person must commit himself wholly, and the new member feels an emotional uplift that reflects both the reception of grace and the seriousness of conversion. The community stands witness. Baptists are now the largest denomination in the United States, infinitely fragmented and periodically recombined. The Southern Baptist convention is the most powerful of these confederations. Today it is second only to the Catholic Church.

Protestantism and Politics

In the Genevan system, divine law ultimately but not directly governs civil power. Pastors influence magistrates but are not themselves magistrates. In New England, the Saints control impure society and constrain it to obey their interpretation of the divine will. They are only 8% of the population, but they run the village assemblies and they alone elect magistrates, whom they expect to punish sinners. They are not tolerant. Before independence, it is London that protects dissidents and maintains a certain pluralism, but only for Protestants. Pennsylvania is more flexible and Virginia, an aristocratic society, still more so.

It is Virginians, more deistic than Christian, who draft history's first secular constitution. Authority does not come from God, but from the consent of the governed, in fact from white property-owning men. There is no religious test for officers of the federal state. An officer can choose between a religious "oath" and a nonreligious "affirmation." Nevertheless, until the end of the nineteenth century, policies in the states limit access to official positions to Protestants alone.

The state is secular, but without secularism. It does not form moral men; it is because citizens are moral that free institutions can endure. The Calvinists think that the "godless" Constitution is an "original sin." The Baptists accommodate themselves better to it. They helped to ratify this Constitution, but they do not renounce their efforts to convert the democratic community into an evangelical community. All agree on sacralizing the constitutional texts as a kind of compensation for the absence of any sacred reference. In this way national unity is affirmed with the help of a millenarian mystique. "A single providential narrative covers the discovery of America, the Protestant Reformation, the Pilgrim fathers and the founding fathers, the Puritan covenant, government by contract, the conquest of the American territory and the coming of the Kingdom" (Richet). School books offer a mix of religion, morality, and civic education. Bible-reading in the schools is a public exercise of devotion, still reinforced by prayer and by the recitation of Psalms. The election of Saints thus passes on to the elect nation. The City upon a Hill is vindicated by the Manifest Destiny of the United States. "God cannot do without America," declared Matthew Simpson, Methodist bishop and confidant of Lincoln, in 1853. This is echoed by President Eisenhower a century later: "Our government has no sense unless it is founded in a deeply felt religious faith, and I don't care what it is."

A lot happened between these two declarations.

The Trials of the Nineteenth Century

The fusion of national sentiment and religious feeling left out many Americans. Native Americans, Blacks, Jews, and Catholics had no place in it. The divide between the North and the South only got worse. When the Civil War began, southern and northern partisans had difficulty agreeing on the meaning of their common Protestant faith. On both sides the identification between religion and nation was more absolute than ever, but these were two different nations, now enemies. In his Second Inaugural Address, Lincoln declared: "Both read the same Bible and pray to the same God, and each invokes His aid against the other. ... The prayers of both could not be answered" (Richet). The South modifies the preamble of the Constitution so as to invoke "the favor and guidance of Almighty God." The northern churches would like to do the same, but Lincoln does not follow them. In his famous Gettysburg address the nation is put "under God," but he confirms the secular principle of "government of the people, by the people, for the people."

After the defeat, the religious tone is somber in the southern states. The myth of the "Lost Cause" informs a sorrowful, inward-looking Christianity. It revives an old Puritanism, at least as it concerns intolerance and rigorism. This myth opposes the beaten-down South to an ethnically heterogeneous, materialistic North, which is doubly impure, racially and morally. The Ku Klux Klan is part of the mystical wing of the Lost Cause. It draws its imagery from the Bible (the burning cross, the white robes of the Apocalypse) without drawing any objection from preachers. Yankees are the Babylonians of the North, the city of the beast. The Baptism of Blood, which the devastated South has undergone, is also a promise of resurrection, and carries with it the assurance of Christ's return for a reign of a thousand years.

The triumphant North awaits the same millennium. Victory is a sign of its coming. But there is no symmetry. While the South turns inward and long retains its rural character, the North opens itself to all the currents of modernity. The great industrial expansion forces the churches to open their eyes to the social question. Intellectual challenges are no less serious. German philological critique enters into the universities, which have always been less fervent than the masses, and this critique little by little undermines the traditional status of the Bible. Inerrancy is subject to doubts. The practice of opening the Book at random in order to find a verse that, like an oracle, solves life's dilemmas becomes problematic. Darwinism opens up a dispute that has not been resolved.

Melting-Pot

For a long time there was a rallying point for all the churches and sects that came out of the fragmentation of Protestantism: a unanimous hatred of Catholicism. This was one of the most solid legacies of England. But this unifying factor was not sufficient; ethnicity posed an obstacle to the melting-pot.

The abolition of slavery made the formation of a Black church inevitable. Masters somewhat reluctantly baptized their slaves. Slaves were required to attend Sunday worship with their masters, and to learn sermons that taught them obedience and resignation. They could not preach or administer the sacraments. Of course there was no question of accepting them on equal terms with whites in their common assemblies. Blacks therefore formed their own congregations. They remained Christian, but in their own way. Doctrinal orthodoxy was not a concern; often illiterate, they did not have the means to acquire it. They simply expected a new birth, an immediate connection with the divine. Sermons begin informally, build up in power, take on the rhythm of song accompanied by movement, and culminate in a cathartic trance. Is this an African heritage? It is hard to know. Earlier, in the Awakenings and camp meetings, perfectly white Presbyterians and Baptists had known emotional transports of the same type. These Black churches are massively Baptist and Methodist, but with very little attention to doctrine. Catholicism has no impact on them.

Among Protestants, one's country of origin is not forgotten. Lutherans who come from continental Europe remain Germans, Fins, Swedes, and Norwegians. They gather in their own groups. In 1900 there were 24 different Lutheran groups. These groups have better knowledge of doctrine and are involved in theological argument, because intellectual concerns are not foreign to them. A thinker like Niebuhr comes from their ranks.

The same can be said of Jews. The first to arrive came from Germany of the Enlightenment, in which they had participated intensively. They contribute to the founding of a liberal Judaism. These Jews were not very comfortable with the enormous crowds that came from Russia, Poland, and Ukraine, whom they found to be without learning and a little embarrassing. All were in a hurry to become Americans. Still the borders of Judaism remain very clear, even among the most "liberal" of Jews and the most liberal of evangelists. A widespread anti-Semitism enforces this border (Ahlstrom).

By far the most troublesome event was the massive arrival of Catholics. At first discreet and timid, surrounded by a clergy of French émigrés, their numbers grow with the arrival of Bavarians and Austrians, and then acquire the force of a tsunami when the Irish land en masse, fleeing the great famine. Later in the century they will be joined by Italians, Poles, and today by Latinos. All find shelter under the Constitution and official religious liberty, seeking acceptance in a nation that has been and still remains fundamentally Protestant. Today they make up a quarter of Americans, by far the largest of "denominations." One can no longer confine them to outer darkness.

The Protestant reaction was sometimes violent. For a time it succeeded in stopping immigration, prohibiting alcohol, regulating morality, setting limits to Hollywood, forbidding the teaching of Darwinism and affirming creationism in some localities, etc. Such examples of return to the old Puritanism, in the South as in the North, were less religious than nationalist. America for

Americans! The new immigrants' religious power does not only find shelter in federal legislation, which always prevails in the end over opposing state legislation, trial after trial; the immigrants also had to show proof that they were no less national and no less nationalistic than the others. Jews and Catholics approve the war against Spain, as well as the wars of 1917 and 1941, and they are the strongest supporters of Roosevelt and the New Deal. The Cold War was the occasion of a kind of Awakening, a new rise of the Puritan tendency, this time adopted unanimously by all the denominations, who competed with each other in their patriotic zeal.

Evangelism and Fundamentalism

There is a *basso continuo* that accompanies most of the families of American Protestantism: Evangelicalism. This is the common ground shared by Methodists, Baptists, Presbyterians, Disciples of Christ, Pentecostals, etc. It is an interdenominational feature in a "religious market" where more than 265 Main denominations vie for the "clientele." The evangelical spirit inspires Sunday schools, moral crusades, and benevolent works. It is at the heart of Mission. It gives unity to the emotional basis of religious experience.

The evangelical consensus includes the supreme authority of the Bible, salvation through Jesus Christ, and the spiritual transformation of life. G. M. Marsden offered this simple definition of Evangelicalism in the second half of the twentieth century: "whoever likes Billy Graham" (Marsden).

Billy Graham was born in 1918 in North Carolina in a Presbyterian community of the South, right in the Bible Belt. A daily reader of the Bible, he experienced conversion at the age of 16 under the influence of a Baptist preacher. He stayed away from sex until his marriage with a beautiful and intelligent young woman of the Methodist faith, who shared his missionary zeal. He sensed early on his vocation as a preacher. Very soon his exceptional charismatic talents were recognized. President Truman received him in person in 1950. Then he created the Billy Graham Evangelistic

Association, which provided the logistic and material foundation of his enterprise. The new media, radio, film, and television established his international presence. In 1957, he held forth daily, up to the point of physical exhaustion, before crowds of New Yorkers at Madison Square Garden.

A total of 2 million people came to hear him. The televised retransmissions were seen by about 200 million people. "The Bible says" was his motto, his starting point, his hallmark. For the masses he was the representation of "religion," which was made up of commitment, spectacle, moral decision, biblical piety, and hope for redemption (Richet).

Billy Graham preached for almost 60 years. His themes were admirably constant. The accent was on conversion conceived as a relation to the word of God of which the Bible is the direct expression. Before, there is inward death, sin, and the threat of eternal damnation. After, there is the seal of grace, the new life. The core of conversion is found in faith in Jesus Christ, the son of God, the Savior who took sins upon him on the cross and, henceforth, the Lord who directs the life of the Christian. His rhetoric, in the tradition of the Awakenings, enlivens the human anguish of living under the Empire of Evil and of death. Billy Graham is inexhaustible on the vanity of human beings' attempt to save themselves by their own efforts. He believes in the images of the Apocalypse and in the approaching end of the world, of which Communism and nuclear terror are the signs: "But we have a code, we truly have a key, we have a sure and certain source of authority. And we find it in the old historic book we call the Bible ...*The Bible Says* ..."

God is holy. He does not tolerate human sin. The devil, who exists, stokes the flames of hell for those who are closed to God's call. But God offers a "second chance," which is conversion, that is, repentance and a new birth. The Bible, which reveals the meaning of history, proves that it is possible. This is a rational fact that moderates the role of emotion and of ecstasy, which are so important in the American tradition. Graham is on good terms with the Pentecostals, but he keeps his distance.

After the brief crisis of conversion, the way is open to the life of sanctification. Alcohol, drugs, and tobacco have no place in it. Daily public prayer and Bible reading find a natural setting in the local church. Thus two key points of Calvinist Protestantism are preserved, individualism and communitarian integration. Sermons conclude with expressions of millenarian hope. "All of history is leading up to this day when Christ will be crowned and will put all enemies beneath his feet." Will this happen soon? Perhaps within 15 years. And the resurrection of the dead? "Just wait for all these tombs to begin bursting like popcorn!"

Preaching is deliberately simple and popular. More sophisticated theologians find this a little simplistic. Karl Barth allows Billy Graham to organize an evangelical campaign in the open air of Basel, warning that no one will come. The meeting takes place; there is a crowd and hundreds of people come forward at the moment of the call to conversion. Niebuhr was of the view that Graham completely neglected social justice; then Graham demonstrated more rigor on the racial question and added an anti-Soviet note to his speeches.

Billy Graham adapted to the evolution of opinion. In his youth, he equated Catholicism with Nazism and Communism as the most dangerous and destructive agents in America. He moderated his critique, and eventually abandoned it entirely. He had cordial relations with John Paul II. These two global personalities worked in tandem, because of their shared charismatic gifts and a certain ecumenical penchant that came out more and more in the "Pope" of American Protestants. This brought Billy Graham closer to the civil rights movement, at least to its moderate wing, because he was aware of the danger of destabilization and mistrusted the activists. Billy Graham, an "interdenominational" Christian, participated fully in the nationalism of the civic religion. He personified national cohesion. "You have touched that part of the American spirit that knows Providence has a grander purpose for our nation." These were Al Gore's words in awarding Graham the Congressional Gold Medal, the greatest honor Congress can grant. He advised Reagan, Nixon, Bush, and Clinton, who listened religiously to the point that it was said that evangelism had entered the White House. He cured G. W. Bush of his alcoholism. He recapitulates the whole story of religion in the United States. He takes up all the themes: the exodus, the chosen people, the Promised Land, a New Jerusalem, the new birth; faith, prayer, individualism, providential universalism, optimism; a pure moral life in conformity with Christ, discipline, self-renunciation. One might also say that, physically, he embodies his country: an attractive bearing, friendly, a bright smile, and robust health almost to the end. When he retires around 2000, Billy Graham *is* America. He dies in 2012.

What is fundamentalism, as opposed to evangelicalism? To reverse Marsden's saying, "fundamentalists are evangelicals who do not like Billy Graham." They find him too open to the liberals who put the inerrancy of the Bible in doubt. They rightly suspect his growing respect for the Catholic Church. They fear the adulteration of good doctrine by heretical elements, such as the worship of the Virgin Mary. They note that his anti-Communism is weakening, and that a social progressivism is entering into his preaching. He is becoming compassionate toward homosexuals, the poor, and victims of all kinds. He does not enter into violent debates for or against Darwinism and creationism. The fundamentalist is a militant, an angry person. But that did not bother half of Americans, among the most conservative of the old Puritan line, who voted in 2012 for a sincere Mormon. Romney openly confessed a non-Christian religion, one that is based upon another Scripture and another doctrine radically incompatible with all traditions stemming from the Bible (Bousquet).

Has fundamentalist anger proven stronger than the Christian instinct? Fifty years ago there were worries surrounding the candidacy of the Catholic John Kennedy. During the campaign of 2012, it was tacitly decided that Mormonism would not be a subject for discussion. Does this mean that political passion as interpreted by the Republican Party has overcome the barrier of the two Protestant principles? Has it in this case erased the clear boundaries surrounding and protecting Protestantism as a whole?

Mission

The nineteenth century was a great century of mission for the United States, as for France and England.

Mission is an essential duty for all tendencies within the evangelical consensus. President McKinley, at the end of the victorious war against Spain (1898), was not sure what to do with the Philippines: "Prayed Almighty God for light and guidance." Finally he was inspired that the only honorable solution was "to educate the Filipinos, and uplift and civilize and Christianize them." He was forgetting that Spain had already done this for three centuries, but in Catholicism, which apparently did not count. Beveridge, a Senator from Indiana, thought that Mission was one of the major duties of the chosen people: Americans "go forth for the healing of the nations. They go forth in the cause of civilization. They go forth for the betterment of man. They go forth, and the word on their lips is Christ and his peace, not conquest and its pillage." Of course one could find declarations no less enthusiastic from Jules Ferry, in a secular spirit, or from Kipling, the poet of the white man, preferably English. The "Manifest Destiny" of the United States held that the civilizing mission combines democracy and religion, and rejects simple territorial conquest.

Today the American mission is carried on by evangelical organizations of Baptist or Methodist inspiration, and often by dissident sects. It is succeeding brilliantly in Latin America, to the point that some predict that Brazil, home of the largest Catholic population in the world, will be Protestant in a few decades. The Marxist mush of "liberation theology" prepared the ground. For its part, the American mission proposes salvation by Jesus Christ and not class struggle, which is something that attracts those Brazilians who are still Christian. This mission benefits from the immense prestige of the dominant nation. To become Protestant is the first step in becoming American.

The Mission has also succeeded in China and in Korea. At night, many bright crosses shine on the roofs of Seoul, representing the various denominations established by the Mission. Better still, the Korean mission has taken the baton from the American mission and has become, after it, the strongest in the world. It operates in China.

The Mission does not fear to attack the Muslim fortress. In this case it is a disadvantage to be an American, given the general hatred of Muslims for the United States. On the other hand, its way of evangelizing is advantageous in comparison to the Catholic mission. It does not suffer from Catholicism's centralized organization, nor does it carry the burden of a unified and obligatory doctrine. The missionary says to Muslims in essence: "you have read the Koran as the uncreated word of God. Here is the Bible: it is a better Scripture, just as much God's word as the other, in which you can put your trust without taking on Catholic complications such as its sacraments and its clergy. Our literalism is not unlike your own. Our iconoclasm and our rejection of alcoholic beverages are also similar. Moreover, you will benefit from the generosity of our churches and from the friendship of the American people."

Reflections

Americans are proud of their religion. They see it as the foundation of their morality, of the good conduct it teaches. This religion has been able to avoid a religious war as well as conflict with the state. It has been a defense against socialism, communism and, now, increasingly, racism. It accords with the well-being of the American people, with its ever-rising standard of living. American preachers have often extolled money-making as a religious duty. Evangelical teaching exalts mutual aid, charitable giving, and solidarity. It still retains responsibility for a large part of the educational and benevolent functions that, in Europe, have been taken from the church and put under the administration of the state. How many hospitals are under the patronage of St. Luke? Is it possible to imagine the grandiose philanthropy of the Carnegies, Rockefeller, J. P. Morgan, Ford, Bill Gates, or Warren Buffet without the inspiration of Calvinist Christianity? The entry into two world wars and the Marshall Plan mobilized the religious spirit, and these great decisions were put almost officially under divine protection.

Max Weber's famous argument in *The Protestant Ethic and the Spirit of Capitalism* has been refuted a thousand times. But it is still valid, because the great books touch the truth in some way.

American Protestantism is not the cause of capitalism (which Weber does not claim in any case), and capitalism now defines itself more in Schumpeter's way than in Weber's. But the fact remains that capitalism is comfortable in America, although for a long time it was not in the southern states, the Bible Belt.

It is said that Protestantism has espoused all the currents of modernity. This is true in general, but it has obstinately resisted moral excesses as soon as they became scandalous. It has even fought against certain scientific theories, such as the theory of evolution, while these have been accepted without much difficulty by Catholics.

It is incontestable that in America there is a connection between Protestantism and the idea of freedom. This connection goes back to the beginnings of the Reformation and to the affirmation of the principle of free inquiry. The Protestant Bible has no notes. Every Christian confronts it directly, in an individual conversation between his conscience and the Word of God. Protestants have at their disposition a number of magnificent translations of the Bible, and every home owns one. In Catholic countries the decrees of the Council of Trent limited the reading of the Bible to authorized persons alone; the same decrees required notes expounding the Catholic Church's interpretation. Up until Vatican II, there was no authorized Bible in the Spanish language. The noble King James Bible has nourished all Americans since the arrival of the Mayflower.

Luther did not found churches, only communities. Since he hoped that, by means of the Reformation, everyone would pass on to a purer City, he left its leadership in the hands of its natural heads, that is, the princes. The prince took on the functions of the Bishop. This was not favorable to democracy. Calvinists, for their part, proposed an alternative model of the church, with no Bishop and independent of the Prince, where the people would have something to say along with pastors, teachers, and elders. In New

England, Calvinism prepared the way for democracy. Religious authority was held by Presbyterian synods, but their control was supple. And the communities broke free of them as they were authorized to do by Congregationalist doctrine. Each community elected its own pastor and chose its liturgy and hymns. And since local magistrates shared the same "persuasion," there was a mutual exchange, under shared religious principles and the common law. The linkage between Protestantism, political freedom, democracy and equality before the law seems to be well-established by historians. This does not exclude outbreaks of fanaticism at certain times and in certain places.

Catholicism is not as monolithic as its adversaries think. Throughout its long history it has known various sensibilities and theological schools. It is crystallized in numerous religious congregations that are not always friends. The relationships between Dominicans, Franciscans, and the Jesuits have been difficult. But the Roman "judge of peace" maintains coexistence among these elements within the same church. In America, the nuances and interpretations are generally supported by charismatic pastors not beholden to any superior authority. This is the source of the fragmentation that Europeans find so surprising, the crumbling into innumerable denominations that still does not destroy religious unity.

In effect all have remained faithful to the heritage and all are right to call themselves Protestants. Creation *ex nihilo*, original sin, salvation by Jesus Christ—these beliefs are accepted by all parties. To this we can add the Protestant principles: *sola gratia, sola fide, sola scriptura*. Despite the difference of emphasis between Jonathan Edwards' preaching and that of Billy Graham, I see no rupture, but on the contrary a fidelity that has lasted for two centuries.

The third Protestant principle, *sola scriptura*, has had different effects in Europe and in America. Luther had an existential conception of Christianity. The act of faith had liberated him all at once from the unbearable anguish that tormented him. This transformation had rendered his scholastic and philosophical education worthless, since he had experienced its impotence. But anxiety can return, and this is why it was necessary, in Lutheran countries, to have recourse to speculation, to a philosophy of another kind, in order, so to speak, to justify justification. Things were different in Calvinist countries. Once conversion under the influence of grace is attained, and this is immediate, the Calvinist framework requires the believer to enter in to the sanctification of life. Sanctification involves personal responsibility and is accomplished through work. Living virtuously and diligently, the Puritan has no time for speculation.

He has no need for it. "The Bible says ..." The Book provides a code, Billy Graham preached, a key, a ready solution for every situation in life. For the Puritan, the man in a hurry, who is busy with useful things and always lacking something, biblical religion allows for considerable economies where thinking is concerned. This is why one does not see the birth of a grand theology, but rather of bursts of feeling, preaching, and crusades led by pastors or charismatic personalities. A few thinkers bring in new reflections, generally directly related to practice, but their voices are rarely heard beyond the United States. Theological essentials are contained in the Bible, and in the early writings of the Reformation, and this is sufficient. Theological learning is often limited to examining and re-examining the sacred book, in going deeper into its exegesis in order to determine "what Christ really said." "Variations" in interpretation are not very significant; they are accepted and do not threaten the overall unity.

The sacralization of Scripture, the idea of "traceability," is thought to be a safeguard against visionary excesses, such as the Catholic temptation. But it also stifles intellectual life. This is why, where religion is concerned, the emphasis is more and more on emotion. It is emotion that is required for conversion, which gives access to baptism and to communion. The inward turn is produced, through grace, by the eloquent words of the pastor, by the extraordinary talent of a Whitefield in earlier times or of a Billy Graham yesterday. Doctrine does not change, but souls are shaken, healed, and progress toward salvation. Christian life is not theoretical but practical. Conversion is judged by its results. The general empiricism of the country is satisfied.

The lesser importance accorded to doctrinal orthodoxy, the primacy of experience, of good conduct, of piety, of "good deeds," eliminates internal borders. Within Protestantism the evangelical movement little by little comes to dominate, to become the reference point and center of gravity.

This can be seen in the manner of prayer. Americans pray publicly, to the surprise of Europeans. Family meals begin with grace. Important meetings, even in the White House, begin with prayer. Confessional differences become unimportant. Catholics are invited and do not avoid the invitation. "Let us pray." Everyone is reverently silent. What makes up this prayer, what is it about? That is the business of the individual. This is never the neutral and empty voluntary reverence of French ceremonies, the "minute of silence." One prays to God.

Public prayer is also where we see a sign of the national religion. Allegiance to the nation, to its institutions, its Constitution, and its unity are intimately intermingled with prayer addressed to God. Common prayer momentarily unifies the denominations thought to be strangers to the spirit of America, classified as "un-American," as Catholicism and Judaism once were and as Islam is today. In common prayer, America's openness, her generosity toward the immigrant and her hospitality show forth the Christian meaning of a blessing.

Perspectives

At first confined to the original thirteen colonies, the religious market today has grown to a global scale. It is marked by the rapid success of the evangelical movement, which offers itself by breaking up into various "brands." In the United States, the older denominations are losing ground, especially the Presbyterian synods and Episcopalianism. It is very easy and altogether acceptable to change denominations over the course of a life, just for convenience, because the local pastor, whether Methodist or Baptist, offers a more attractive "program."

The evangelical movement has penetrated the Church of England. It gets along with all of its branches, High, Low, and Broad.

The King James Bible has been retranslated into modern English. This Church was famous for its knowledge, its patristic learning, and the beauty of its language. One wonders what evangelical simplification will leave of this august monument. About half of French Protestantism has gone over to the Baptists, often in an extreme form— Pentecostal, Adventist, Darbyist, etc.

The Catholic Church therefore finds itself on the defensive. In the United States it had seen enormous progress mainly for demographic reasons, since there were never massive conversions. It grew by the addition of waves of Germans, Irish, southern Italians, Poles, Hispanics, and Canadians. It was not easily accepted. Until recently its leadership was Irish. It is important to remember that the priests of Ireland, and its future bishops, were educated in French seminaries, particularly that of Saint-Omer, a Jansenist stronghold. This explains the rigorous tone of American Catholicism, which sometimes makes it resemble the Presbyterians in its moral views. Like them, American Catholics are tempted by Congregationalist dispersion.

And yet they have held back. The chain that links them with Rome has never been broken. One of the major motives for the long-held practice of excluding Catholics was that they "obey the Pope," an argument which forced them to demonstrate their zeal as good citizens and their irreproachable patriotism in all circumstances.

Still, the Catholic type of Christianity is very different. It is fundamentally intellectual, theoretical, and doctrinal. It also produces religious emotions, but not as a proof. Proof comes instead through the practice of the sacraments, which are numerous and binding. It is the sacraments, and not simple meditation on the Bible, that assures communication with God. The Eucharist takes the realism of the divine presence further than the Calvinist Holy Supper. Penitence offers a form of liberation from sin that is more objective and certain than Protestant repentance, an affair between the believer and God. It is renewable, whereas Calvinist justification is given once and for all. At the same time, the sacraments put the priest in a key position. One does not attain the status of a pastor by receiving an inner call; beyond this, the future priest must receive long instruction and training in a separate institution, and finally be ordained only by a bishop. As for the orthodoxy of thought, it is based on doctrine. This is an immense and ancient cathedral, at once theological and philosophical, whose solidity requires constant attention, because it can crumble. One cannot remove an element without compromising the coherence of the whole and risking its collapse.

It is understandable that Catholicism can horrify Protestants. This is because of certain doctrinal elements (the assumed worship of Mary, for example), but especially because it attacks the supreme value, freedom. It is a cause of oppression because of its hierarchical structure, and it is a cause of foolishness, it is thought, because its obligatory beliefs are supposed to limit freedom of thought.

The divide between Catholicism and evangelical Protestantism is therefore profound. But how is it possible that Catholics have been able to make such progress in American society? Today an institution as sacred as the Supreme Court does not contain a single Protestant Justice. It is more or less equally divided between Catholics and Jews. Is this progress in tolerance? Is it proof of a religious and intellectual opening? Certainly. But there are other elements to consider that are consequences of the vast revolution of the 1960s.

The first signs of change appeared in the nearly simultaneous rise of the civil rights movement and of the Vatican II Council. These years, the 1960s and 1970s of the twentieth century, were "an axial moment." Much changed in the social and moral order. Certain very ancient institutions, well older than the Bible, such as marriage, for example, were contested. Established authorities, and the idea of authority itself, were overthrown. The family, the school, the university, the hospital, business, and even the military had to redefine themselves.

This vast revolution is ongoing and we do not know where it will lead us, for it is not finished. It is possible to look at it as a religious movement. As things stand now, some of its early results can be described. Let us limit ourselves to the United States.

It is far from certain that the "American exception" can be sustained indefinitely. Cells characterized by irreligion and free thought grow along with the development of mass education and particularly of higher education. It is in the universities that opposition to religious conformism began. The Calvinist concentration on the Bible and its exegesis can turn against itself. The "historical-critical method" undermines the conviction of inerrancy and literal interpretation. Individual charity has turned into social concern and philanthropy, and the administration of the neutral state takes over more and more. The doctrinal question, which was never foremost, becomes a secondary concern, then obsolete and even a matter of indifference. Christianity withdraws little by little from the public sphere. School prayer, Sabbath observance, abstinence, continence and sexual discipline decline spectacularly. State secularism relegates religion to the private sphere. Religion still publicly accompanies the great social movements, the struggle for racial equality and for women's rights, but these movements do not in themselves call for the affirmation of a confessional identity. Morality suffices, and as Jules Ferry said, morality is neither secular nor Christian but simply moral. Evangelical faith becomes more subjective and emotional than ever.

This might have been an opportunity for the Catholic Church, a guardian of theology and of the intellectual life of the faith and sentinel of true doctrine. But it seems that this church is undergoing a parallel and concomitant devolution. This cannot be attributed to the pressure of the majority religion, because one sees the same thing in Europe as well. The last time it made concessions to American influence was at the time of the heresy called "Americanist," which Rome immediately struck down (1899). This time the impulse has come from the inside.

I do not wish to describe the crisis of the Catholic Church and of Protestantism, but rather the global emergence of a substantially different religion, which I will call the religion of humanity.

This religion encompasses Christian elements and gives them a different meaning. It includes the equality of all human beings, whatever their race (if this word still exists), their social rank, their religion, their nationality, their natural gifts, etc. Human beings are rights-bearers, and these rights are already enumerated in the American Bills of Rights and, with more emphasis, in the French Declaration of the Rights of Man and the Citizen. These rights—and the list gets longer every year—have been approved by the Catholic Church for the last 50 years. It is now possible to speak of a sacralized doctrine of human rights.

The religion of humanity is associated with "democracy." This concept is easier to proclaim than to define. Every political regime in the world calls itself democratic, notably those which are less so, because today only democracy can claim political legitimacy. The United States believes that it represents it in its purity and that it is part of its mission to spread it universally. The Catholic Church likewise has supported representative democracy since the Second World War.

The religion of humanity is relativistic. It is convinced that there is no established truth and that all religions are equivalent, equal in dignity, and worthy of respect, and that a person can find his spiritual good, his salvation, in any one of them. Relativism is the ultimate form of an ecumenism "without borders." Pope Benedict XVI opposed relativism with all his strength, but the movement appears to be irresistible.

This religion is pacifist and compassionate. Nothing in the past is more regrettable than the Crusades, persecutions, and discrimination. In the case of war, one must not kill anyone, even and especially enemies—for there are no enemies and it is intrinsically evil to have any.

Thus all the old varieties of the Christian religion find themselves absorbed and drowned in the new religion. This religion dissolves their forms and obliterates their distinctive shapes. Catholic teachings evaporate along with Protestant principles. The old Christianity as a whole is everywhere the object of mockery and of indignation.

The progress of the religion of humanity has been rapid, but uneven. It is held back by the figure of nationalism. In the United States, a group as strange as the Mormons is successful because it represents American values such as hard work and the familiar prohibitions, as well as an extreme nationalism: according to the Mormon Bible, the lost tribes of Israel were the first immigrants, and Jesus personally visited the American territory. Thus, even though it is clearly non-Christian, the Mormon Church was seen by Obama's partisans as well as by Romney's as "just another denomination." "The Church of Jesus Christ of Latter-Day Saints" refuses nonetheless to be dissolved into the humanitarian magma, but the religion of humanity takes no account of it. In Europe the religion of humanity welcomes Islam and is surprised when it remains faithful to the religion of the Koran. It holds out hope that Islam will in the end become part of its own religiosity. Where can one establish a border, if humanitarianism refuses to see it?

I will stop here. My subject was American Protestantism and we are leaving it behind, as we are Christianity in general.